Pacific Northwest SALMON

C O O K B O O K

Curt & Margie Smitch
Ron & Ellie Wagner

NORTHWEST RESOURCES
Olympia, Washington

Library of Congress Catalog Card Number
85-5058
ISBN 0-9614579-0-2

To order copies of the *Pacific Northwest
Salmon Cookbook,* send $9.95 plus $1.50
for postage and handling (Washington
residents add $.78 sales tax) to: Northwest
Resources, 1617 East Bay Drive, Olympia,
WA 98506.

Production: Backwater Corporation

Consultant, Editorial Assistance:
   Gail Nelson

Art Direction, Art: Dethlefs & Associates

Word Processing: Bobbie Taylor

Typesetting: The Franklin Press

Cover photo courtesy of Alaska Seafood
   Marketing Institute

Back cover photo by David Niedopytalski

Library of Congress Cataloging in Publication Data
Main entry under title:

Pacific Northwest salmon cookbook.

   Includes index.
   1. Cookery (Salmon)   I. Smitch, Curt, 1944-
TX747.P33   1985   641.6'92   85-5058
ISBN 0-9614579-0-2 (pbk.)

Printed in U.S.A.

This book is dedicated to those special persons in our lives who enrich life itself: Dawn Smitch, a daughter whose smile fills all hearts; Carolyn Hansen Butler, whose memory reminds us daily of what is meant by friendship, beauty, motherhood and humanity; Grace and Pappy Hartman, whose selfless friendship convinced Ron and Ellie to make their home in Olympia.

ACKNOWLEDGMENTS

There are numerous people we would like to thank for their parts in making this book a reality:

All of our friends who chose to share their favorite salmon dishes with us, and thus shared their special affection for the salmon. And those same friends and others who joined us on Tuesday evenings for over a year to test recipes.

Merle and Anne Dowd, whose encouragement and assistance have made our first publishing experience a rewarding one.

Gail Nelson, for her devotion to this book, her publishing savvy, her ever-present enthusiasm, and her editorial assistance.

Bobbie Taylor, whose perfection in typing and retyping of numerous drafts enabled us to move forward.

Pam Blakely, who so kindly provided her typing services when a second typist was needed.

Deb Dethlefs, whose creativity in design and layout so beautifully complemented our text.

CONTENTS

INTRODUCTION

The Pacific Northwest Salmon Cookbook is a special collection of outstanding salmon recipes.

*F*rom tantalizing hors d'oeuvres to savory bouillabaisse to mousse, from smoked to barbecued to baked, the Pacific Northwest Salmon Cookbook offers simple, yet classic, recipes to guarantee your casual brunch, formal dinner or party will be an unforgettable celebration.

Only Curt, Margie, Ron and Ellie could create these truly superior recipes. The subtle blends and daring combinations of ingredients you'll find irresistible are as varied as their passions for the salmon.

Curt, an avid fisherman and assistant to the director of the Washington State Department of Fisheries, believes a salmon feast pays homage to the salmon's niche in nature. He delights in telling the incredible story of the salmon's perilous journey: Surviving dams, floods and predators, it swims from its freshwater birthplace to the vast ocean. There a sudden biochemical metamorphosis occurs in the salmon, enabling it to feed and grow in an otherwise hostile saltwater environment. Finally, two to four years later and after a journey of thousands of miles, the survivors return to the river of their birth. Fat, fit and frantic, they begin the upstream race back to their gravel birthplace. There, exhausted by the journey, the salmon die, but only after they pair off and begin the cycle of life anew.

Curt truly believes the sharing of a salmon dinner is, in a real sense, an affirmation that Nature herself is still vigorous and healthy.

Margie, an attorney in the Washington State Attorney General's Office and a gourmet cook, admires the salmon for its well-deserved place in the epicure's hall of fame. Friends and family are frequent guests of Curt and Margie in their *waterfront home, where laughter, salt air, and Margie's flair for salmon are always special treats.*

Ron, a communications specialist, restaurateur, and legislative liaison to the largest sport fishing organization in the State of Washington, discovered his gastronomical interests early in life. Following his heart's desire through the years, he opened restaurants in New York and Olympia, founded an exclusive gourmet catering service, and explored the possibilities of many foods across the country. However, it wasn't until he discovered the infinite versatility and elegance of the salmon that he became a master chef.

Ellie's love affair with the salmon was inspired by her Norwegian grandfather and her family's unusual lifestyle. Living in various lighthouses on the Pacific Coast, they fished for much of their food. Many of the recipes shared in this book are original creations which Ellie, now an administrator in the Department of Retirement Systems, prepared for her family's lighthouse meals.

Whether your passion for salmon began as a fisherman, a cook or a guest, you'll find that whenever fresh salmon graces your table you and your guests will enjoy a connection of friendship, life and nature.

*O*ne salmon goes a long way in the kitchen and is too delicious to waste. Also, it is so versatile that you need not ever serve the same meal twice. Your leftovers will enable you to indulge in a gourmet dish entirely different from the previous day.

The *Pacific Northwest Salmon Cookbook* is designed to allow you to maximize your cooking enjoyment with salmon by transforming your excess salmon into a delicious new main course, vegetable dish, bread, soup, salad or appetizer. Recipes calling for cooked salmon work especially well with leftovers.

SERVE ONLY THE BEST

*W*e're convinced that fresh salmon has a texture, color and flavor that is truly distinctive. These qualities make the difference between an ordinary salmon dinner and one that is exquisite. Therefore, our recipes call for fresh or "fresh frozen" (as described later) salmon that has been properly handled.

Many salmon labeled "fresh" in the markets do not meet our standards. In order to obtain a truly fresh salmon, you should catch it yourself or purchase one with certain qualities described herein.

Following our recipes and guidelines, you will satisfy the most discriminating palate on any occasion.

1

AFTER YOU HOOK IT
BEFORE YOU COOK IT

Selecting the salmon is the most important step in preparing any salmon dish. The second most important step also occurs before cooking begins: Preparing the salmon properly to enhance the flavor.

*I*f you catch the salmon, you are twice blessed. The experience is rewarding, and you can guarantee your fish will be of the finest quality by following these steps:

1. Stun the fish with a sharp blow to the head immediately upon catching it. Do not let the fish flop around in the boat or on shore. Thrashing bruises the flesh and creates a buildup of lactic acids and other metabolic by-products which are harmful to the flesh.

2. Immediately bleed the fish. Studies show that blood in the body of the fish begins to break down tissue within 30 minutes after the fish dies, or sooner in warmer weather. We recommend you cut completely through one gill plate, although some evidence indicates that a deep cut to the backbone, just behind the anal opening, will result in a greater loss of blood. If possible, keep the fish in the net while it is bleeding, and immerse the fish and net in the water. This prevents a mess in your boat and the immediate clotting of the blood, thereby allowing for a greater loss of blood. This is your goal.

    By immediately bleeding your fish, you will extend the freezer life up to six months. Also, you will then have a standard of firmness, color, texture and flavor by which to judge all other salmon, fresh or frozen.

3. After bleeding the fish, place it in ice. The warmer the day, the more critical this becomes. The quicker the body temperature can be reduced to near freezing level, the longer the fish will remain fresh, and the greater will be the freezer life. (Some commercial salmon boats actually install

2

saltwater tanks with temperatures below 30°F in order to reduce the body temperature below the freezing level as quickly as possible without actually freezing the fish.)

Many anglers believe that keeping the fish wet and cool by covering it with a cloth or burlap bag is sufficient, but evidence contradicts this long-held belief. The body temperature should be close to freezing, not cool, in order to slow down the chemical and bacterial breakdown of the flesh. If you want the best, immediately ice your fish.

4. Finally, clean your fish as soon as possible, particularly if the fish is not iced and the weather is warm. The acids in the stomach do not lose their potency when the fish dies. The warmer the body temperature of the fish, the quicker these chemicals seep through the stomach and begin to break down the tissue. In addition, cleaning the fish before it sits too long increases the amount of blood lost, since the stomach and surrounding area are extremely rich in blood vessels.

Cleaning Salmon

If possible, obtain a cutting board longer than the salmon, or stack two or three layers of newspaper on the counter and cover them with butcher paper. Place the salmon on its side and insert the tip of a sharp fillet knife in the anal opening and draw the knife toward the head. Once you have opened the stomach cavity from the anal opening to the head, remove the entrails from the salmon cavity.

In most cases, you will want to dispose of the head. Therefore, after removing the entrails, cut behind the pectoral fins toward the top of the head. Simply allow the knife to follow the hard bony "collarbone" that frames the gill opening. Then cut through the backbone and remove the head.

Now that the entrails and head are removed, place the salmon in the sink, head down, and remove the black kidney located along the backbone inside the stomach cavity. (A spoon works nicely for this job.) Then, wash the salmon thoroughly with cold water.

SELECTING
FRESH SALMON

*Y*ou have no way of knowing how a salmon was handled before its arrival at the market. Therefore, you should follow these guidelines to ensure the salmon you purchase is of the highest quality.

When purchasing a fresh salmon, consider these qualities:

SKIN
The skin should be shiny and bright. Indeed, it should gleam and glitter as though the salmon had just jumped out of the water. Stay away from salmon with dull skin lacking the vibrant luster that characterizes a fresh fish.

GILLS
The gills should be a rich dark red. Fish with gills that are beginning to turn pink or are tinged with brown should be examined very carefully.

SCALES
Loss of scales indicates poor handling. Bruised areas lose scales. Soft flesh, indicating improper bleeding or the fact that the body temperature was not reduced soon or low enough, also accounts for scale loss. There is almost nothing good to say about a salmon with more than a few scales missing.

FLESH
The flesh should be firm, yet resilient or elastic when touched. If you make a small indentation in the flesh with your finger, it should spring back to its original shape. Also, stay away from salmon when the flesh readily separates from the bone. This is most apparent when examining the stomach cavity of a dressed salmon.

ODOR

Trust your nose!

The odor of fresh fish is not fishy. It is mild to the olfactory senses. The Federal Food and Drug Administration uses odor as a primary criteria for determining the freshness of fish. They believe that if it smells fishy, something is.

BELLY BURN

Since we do not recommend that you purchase a salmon that has not been cleaned, even though the fish market might advertise it as fresh, it is important to check the stomach cavity of a dressed salmon. If the examination reveals dark discoloration, soft flesh and bones that easily separate from the surrounding flesh, you can assume that the fish was not properly handled. Leave such a fish for someone else.

SELECTING FROZEN SALMON

*A*gain, it is impossible to determine the manner in which salmon was handled before it was frozen. Therefore, you must rely on established brand names, on trial and error, and basic guidelines.

When purchasing frozen fish, ask yourself these questions:

- Is it firm and frozen solid?·

- Does the fish appear to be dried out, or does it have a nice, glossy appearance? Are there white spots or brittle, thin edges on the fins?

- Is the flesh discolored?

- Is there frost on the package? A thick layer of frost indicates that the fish has been frozen too long, or that changes in temperature have occurred.

Avoid frozen fish that exhibit any of these signs. And remember, you cannot refreeze a fresh fish. You can freeze a frozen fish again after it's cooked, but only for a short time.

PERFECT FILLETS AND STEAKS

The key to filleting your salmon is taking your time and using a sharp fillet knife. First, make a cut along the backbone from the head end to the tail. Make sure you have cut down to the backbone. Next, pull the flesh away from the fish and, using the tip of the knife, carefully cut along the rib cage. Working slowly, you will "peel" the flesh away from the rib cage, leaving you with a beautiful, boneless fillet. Use the same procedure on the opposite side.

Salmon are easily cut into steaks with a sharp knife. Begin at the head and cut cross sections approximately 1 inch thick.

FROZEN SALMON

Frozen salmon can be a gourmet's delight.

Frozen salmon, although never quite as rich in flavor as fresh salmon, can be a gourmet's delight, if frozen properly. This applies to home freezing as well as to commercially frozen salmon.

Some authorities believe a fish should be frozen within 8 to 10 hours after it has been killed. They

6

assume, however, that the fish was packed in ice or stored in the refrigerator during the time prior to freezing. Our experience indicates that you can store your fish in the refrigerator or keep it on ice up to 24 hours and still have a quality frozen fish, as long as the fish is properly handled, as we described earlier.

Under no circumstances should you freeze a salmon that has been previously frozen and thawed. Nor do we recommend that you freeze salmon that is purchased from a fish market or store. It is simply impossible to tell how fresh it actually is.

Freezing Your Own

We have found a simple and inexpensive way to freeze whole and dressed salmon or fillets for up to six months without losing its freshness:

Completely wrap the fish in paper towels, then thoroughly wet the towels with cold water. Next, wrap the fish in two layers of newspaper and completely wet the newspaper with cold water. Finally, wrap the entire "package" in heavy-duty aluminum foil. Mark the date and species of salmon, and it's ready for the freezer.

You can also freeze steaks this way. However, we have found that steaks do better in milk cartons filled with water if you are going to keep them in the freezer longer than four months.

In all cases, try to keep your home-frozen salmon at a constant temperature of at least 0°F (-18°C). Colder temperatures are even better.

Fresh Frozen Fish

We mentioned "fresh frozen" earlier, in regard to quality fish. The term has come to denote fish that are killed, cleaned, bled and immediately immersed in a super-cooled brine bath (below 32°F) and then blast frozen at temperatures below 0°F (-18°C). After this has occurred, the fish is sprayed with a water mist which forms a frozen water "envelope" around it. This is done several times until the fish is completely covered with a layer of ice ⅛ to ⅜ of an inch thick. The fish is then stored in a freezer at -15°F (-28°C) or under.

The key to this process, and the reason why it is

called "fresh frozen", relates to the way in which the fish is handled after it is killed, and how quickly the body temperature is lowered to the freezing level.

THAWING SALMON

*F*or best results, your salmon should be covered with plastic wrap or foil, placed in a shallow pan or tray, and left in a refrigerator to thaw for approximately 24 hours. It may also be thawed in a microwave oven according to manufacturer's directions.

Use thawed salmon as soon as possible, for optimum flavor and quality.

SMOKE YOUR OWN

*O*ne can easily run out of superlatives to describe the virtues of smoked salmon. Whether it is used to enhance a tray of hors d'oeuvres, to add special flavor to a favorite recipe, or simply served as a snack with cold beer, smoked salmon is an all-time favorite.

Smoked salmon is accurately described as a delicacy. Like all delicacies, it is expensive to buy. So, if you want to save money and impress your friends, we recommend you smoke your own salmon.

The smoking process described in our recipes is simple. Years of experimentation have proven that the procedure can be adjusted to fit your lifestyle. So if you are too busy to add wood chips to the smoker or to take the fish out of the brine precisely on time, don't panic. As long as you have used the specified ingredients, your friends will still remark that yours is some of the best smoked salmon they've ever tasted!

NUTRITIONAL VALUE

*E*xperts agree that salmon contains protein, vitamins and minerals which are essential to your diet. It's low in calories and, according to new studies, may actually reduce the risk of coronary heart disease.

Salmon is one of the few irresistible foods that are nutritionally good too.

Consider these benefits:

PROTEIN

Your body needs amino acids for proper growth and maintenance. The source of amino acids is protein. Salmon is an excellent source of protein. In fact, as a source of protein, salmon ranks second only to eggs.

MINERALS

Salmon contains a number of minerals that are essential to the proper functioning of the body. It has been identified as a good source of iodine, calcium, copper, iron, potassium, magnesium, phosphorus, and sodium. Interestingly, contrary to what many people assume, salmon is lower in sodium than other foods such as beef, pork and lamb. This makes salmon an ideal choice for people on low- salt diets.

VITAMINS

Salmon is a good source of several essential vitamins, particularly vitamins A, D, B-6 and B-12. It also contains small amounts of vitamin C.

FATS

Most of us are aware that we should reduce our

intake of saturated fats and substitute unsaturated fats. Saturated fats, found primarily in animal tissue, are thought to contribute to the buildup of cholesterol in the blood, which increases the chance of a heart attack or stroke. It is believed that unsaturated fats, found primarily in vegetable oils, do not contribute to cholesterol buildup in the blood.

Salmon provides double benefits with regard to fats. First, salmon is lower in fat content than red meats. And second, the fat contained in salmon is highly unsaturated. In fact, recent research has identified salmon as one of the two (mackerel is the other) major sources of eicosapentanoic acid, a unique fatty acid thought to lower serum cholesterol and serum triglyceride levels in the blood. These reductions lower the chance of coronary heart disease.

CALORIES AND CARBOHYDRATES

Salmon is lower in calories than beef and poultry. It contains little or no carbohydrates. This makes salmon an excellent food for those who wish to limit calorie intake while obtaining essential vitamins, minerals and protein.

SALMON SPECIES

*P*acific salmon account for six of the seven species of anadromous salmon — salmon which spend part of their life in fresh water and part in salt water. They are normally found in the northern hemisphere, ranging from the temperate zone to the Arctic Circle. However, in recent years, some species have been successfully introduced into South America and South Africa. In addition, both Coho and Chinook salmon were introduced into the Great Lakes in 1966 and have experienced

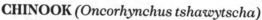

tremendous success in this totally freshwater environment.

There is one species of anadromous Atlantic salmon.

Below are brief descriptions of each of the species, as well as a general comment on the respective food quality. In our opinion, the flavor of all salmon is good if the salmon is properly cared for and prepared.

CHINOOK *(Oncorhynchus tshawytscha)*

The Chinook salmon, also known as King, Tyee, Spring, Tule, and Blackmouth (a sexually immature salmon), is the largest of the Pacific salmon. Fish exceeding 100 pounds have been recorded, although the average weight is closer to 22 pounds. They are found from the Sacramento River in California to the northernmost waters of Alaska. Their life span is normally four to seven years.

The Chinook has spotted blue-green back and spots covering the tail. The lower gums are black. The flesh, which ranges in color from deep salmon to white, is rich in oils and separates into large flakes when cooked. It is among the most delicious of salmon and is truly "king" of the dinner table.

SOCKEYE *(Oncorhynchus nerka)*

The Sockeye, also called Red or Blueback, ranges from the Columbia River to Alaska, with a particularly large and well-known run in Canada's Fraser River. The slimmest of the Pacific salmon, its weight rarely exceeds 14 pounds. The average weight is five to seven pounds. Sockeye live four to six years and have the unique characteristic of living for at least one year in a freshwater lake.

The Sockeye has large glassy eyes and is shaded blue-green on its back, hence the name Blueback. However, upon returning to the rivers, both the males and females turn deep red with dark greenish heads, hence the name Reds. Spots are absent from the back and tail. The flesh is deep red and firm in texture.

Many people consider the flavor of Sockeye superior to other salmon.

PINK *(Oncorhynchus gorbuscha)*
The smallest of the Pacific salmon with an average weight of five pounds, the Pink or Humpy (named for the prominent cartilaginous hump on the back of male Pinks) ranges from the Klamath River in California to Asia. The Pink's two-year life cycle distinguishes it from other Pacific salmon. It is the most abundant species of salmon in the north Pacific.
Pink salmon have tiny scales and large oval spots on the back and tail. The flesh is a delicate pink color. It contains less oils than Sockeye or Chinook, and breaks into small pieces when cooked. The Pink salmon is usually considered to be of lesser value than the other Pacific salmon.

COHO *(Oncorhynchus kisutch)*
The Coho or Silver salmon is smaller than the Chinook. The average weight is eight to nine pounds, but fish over 30 pounds have been recorded. The Coho ranges from as far south as Monterey, California to the Bering Sea in the north. It usually lives for three years and is well known for the extremely rapid growth that occurs in the last year. The Coho is lightly spotted on the back and upper tail, which is more squarish than other salmonid tails. The gums of the Coho are white and easily distinguished from the black tongue. The flesh is a deeper, richer salmon color than the Chinook and forms large flakes with excellent texture when cooked. Its flavor is equal to that of the Chinook.

CHUM *(Oncorhynchus keta)*
The Chum salmon has an extensive range. It is found from the Puget Sound to northern Alaska, in Asia and Japan. In fact, Chums are most abundant in Asian rivers. Russians refer to them as Nerka, while the Japanese call them Sake. They are also known as Dogs, because of the large fang-like teeth that are present during the spawning season.

Chum salmon live three to five years and generally weigh eight to 10 pounds, although they have been recorded at over 30 pounds. Chum closely resemble Sockeye, but are larger. A white tip on the anal fin and faint grid-like shading on the sides readily distinguish this species. The flesh is white to pink and lower in oils than other species. When cooked, the texture is course.

MASU *(Oncorhynchus masu)*

This species of salmon, native to the rivers of the Hokkaido islands in Japan and off the coast of Manchuria, is not usually found in North America. It is small, averaging four to eight pounds, and closely resembles the Coho. You are unlikely to find Masu, also known as Cherry, salmon in local stores or fish markets. If you do cook with Masu, treat it as you would treat Coho.

ATLANTIC SALMON *(Salmo salar)*

The Atlantic salmon ranges from Maine and eastern Canada to the European coast. The average weight falls between 15 and 25 pounds. The largest Atlantic salmon on record, approximately 100 pounds, was captured in a net near Norway.

Like the Pacific salmon, it is bright silver with spots along a greenish-blue colored back. However, some biologists believe it is actually more closely related to the trout family, *Salmo,* than to the Pacific salmon, *Oncorhynchus.* Indeed, many Steelhead fishermen, upon seeing an Atlantic salmon, are startled by its close resemblance to the great sea-going Rainbow trout, *Salmo gairdneri,* the Steelhead.

APPETIZERS

Salmon Dip

Mix all ingredients until well blended and chill. Serve with your favorite fresh vegetables, chips or crackers.

3 hard-boiled eggs, mashed
1 cup smoked salmon, flaked
1 teaspoon vinegar
2 tablespoons mayonnaise
3 tablespoons pimiento, chopped
  salt and pepper to taste

Gravlox

Combine sugar, salt and dill. Coat the salmon and place salmon skin side down in a baking dish.

Refrigerate 3 to 4 days, turning every day. Keep covered.

Rinse salmon in cold water and pat dry. Slice paper thin and serve with a selection of bread and mustards.

For variety salmon can be marinated with ¼ cup cognac and ¼ cup dry white wine.

2-4 pounds of salmon fillets, with skin
2 cups sugar
2 cups salt
1 tablespoon dill

Salmon Cheese Ball

Finely flake smoked salmon. Blend together with remaining ingredients. Shape into ball.

Roll in chopped nuts or parsley if desired. Serve with crackers.

This salmon ball freezes beautifully.

4 cups smoked salmon
1 8-ounce package cream cheese
1 cup sour cream
1 teaspoon salt
1 teaspoon pepper
  pinch tarragon
¼ cup chopped onion
1 tablespoon lemon juice

Salmon Cheese Spread

Mix all ingredients until well blended and chill. Serve with crackers or as a vegetable dip.

1 cup smoked salmon, flaked
1 onion, finely chopped
3 tablespoons mayonnaise
1 5-ounce jar pimiento cheese spread
dash Worcestershire sauce

Salmon Leipschen

Prepare Madeira Sauce according to directions on page 152.

Cook spinach thoroughly, adding vinegar and bacon. Drain and set aside.

Cook sausage balls in a small amount of vegetable oil. Turn frequently until brown and well done. Remove from skillet and drain on a paper towel.

Place 3 sausage balls and 1/4 cup salmon on each shell. Cover sausage and salmon with 2 tablespoons sauce. Evenly divide spinach and lay atop sauce. Cover spinach with 2 tablespoons sauce. Place shells in a 350° oven and bake 15 minutes. Remove from oven and cover each shell with whipped cream. Place under broiler for 1 additional minute. Serve immediately.

Serves 8.

2   10-ounce packages frozen chopped spinach
1   teaspoon vinegar
3   tablespoons crumbled bacon
2   cups cooked salmon, broken into bite-size pieces
1   pound ground sausage, formed into 24 balls
    vegetable oil
2   cups Madeira Sauce
2   cups whipped cream
8   scallop shells

Apple, Cheese and Salmon Platter

Slice apples, cheese and salmon; arrange slices on serving platter. Serve with Dill Dip.

smoked salmon
apples
cheddar cheese
Dill Dip (below)

Dill Dip

Combine mayonnaise, sour cream, dill weed and garlic powder. Let chill several hours.

½ cup mayonnaise
½ cup sour cream
1 heaping tablespoon dill weed
dash of garlic powder

Smoked Salmon Stuffed Eggs

Cut peeled eggs in half lengthwise. Slip out egg yolks and mash with fork. Mix in remaining ingredients. Cover and chill.

Fill egg whites with salmon mixture. Garnish with paprika.

½ cup smoked salmon, minced
¼ cup sour cream
¼ cup mayonnaise
1 tablespoon lemon juice
salt and pepper to taste
6 hard-boiled eggs

Lomilomi Salmon

Combine salmon, salt and lemon juice. Cover and chill for 12 hours.

Drain and rinse salmon. Cover salmon with cold water and soak for several hours. Change water several times.

Mix salmon with the remaining ingredients. Squeeze the mixture using your fingers until the mixture is blended and homogenous. Cover and chill for several hours. Serve on bed of lettuce leaves.

Lomi is the Hawaiian word for massage.

1 1-pound skinned salmon fillet, cut in small chunks
6 tablespoons coarse salt
1/4 cup lemon juice
5 tomatoes, peeled and chopped
1 sweet onion, minced
2 green onions including tops, minced

Pickled Salmon

Combine pickling spice, vinegar, water, salt, and sugars in a saucepan and boil slowly for 20 minutes. Strain and add chopped onions and salmon. Place into a covered jar and refrigerate.

3 tablespoons pickling spice
1 cup vinegar
1 cup water
1 tablespoon salt
1/4 cup brown sugar
1/4 cup white sugar
2 onions, chopped
2 salmon fillets, broiled and chunked

Smoked Salmon Horseradish Dip

Finely flake the salmon and set aside. Mix together the remaining ingredients. Add salmon and chill 6 hours before serving. Serve with crackers or chips.

1/2 cup smoked salmon, flaked

1 3-ounce package cream cheese, softened

2 tablespoons sour cream

2 tablespoons mayonnaise

1 tablespoon finely chopped onion

2 tablespoons horseradish

1/8 teaspoon garlic powder

salt and pepper to taste

Salmon Crispies

Place butter and cheese in bowl. Let stand at room temperature until soft. Mix butter, cheese and salmon until smooth. Add flours, cayenne and mix well. Stir in rice crispies. Roll into 1-inch balls.

Bake on ungreased cookie sheet for 12 minutes at 350°. Makes 3 dozen.

This appetizer freezes well. Defrost and serve or wrap in foil and reheat in 350° oven until warm.

1/2 cup butter
4 ounces sharp cheddar cheese, grated
1/3 cup smoked salmon, flaked
1/2 cup self-rising flour
1/2 cup regular flour
cayenne (pinch)
1 cup rice crispies

Salmon Guacamole

Finely flake salmon and set aside. Mix together the remaining ingredients. Add salmon. Chill and serve with tortilla chips.

½ cup smoked salmon
2 avocados, mashed
2 tablespoons sour cream
1 tablespoon green taco sauce, mild
1 tablespoon finely chopped onion
⅛ teaspoon garlic powder
1 teaspoon lemon juice
⅛ teaspoon cayenne

Smoked Salmon, Bacon and Cheddar Rolls

Slice a piece of smoked salmon into ⅛-inch thick, approximately 1-inch long and ½-inch wide pieces; 14 pieces.

Cut each piece of bread and the bacon slices in half. Place a piece of smoked salmon at end of bread and sprinkle with cheese. Roll bread and wrap a piece of bacon around it. Secure with a toothpick.

Place on ungreased cookie sheet and bake at 400° for approximately 15 to 20 minutes or until bacon is done. Serve warm.

smoked salmon
7 slices white bread, crusts removed
4 ounces medium cheddar cheese, shredded
7 slices bacon

Salmon Gueydon

Place fish in a glass bowl. Sprinkle with a generous amount of salt. Combine juice of lemon and limes and vinegar. Pour over fish. Add green pepper and onion. Sprinkle with garlic powder and stir gently. Add water if necessary to completely cover all ingredients.

Refrigerate 4 to 6 hours, stirring occasionally. Drain and serve.

This recipe requires no cooking. The lemon and lime juice "cook" the fish.

2 cups salmon, skinned, boned and cut into bite-size pieces
1 green pepper, cut into strips
1 medium onion, cut into strips
3 limes
1 lemon
1/3 cup white vinegar
   salt
1/2 teaspoon garlic powder

Salmon Spinach Dip

Combine all ingredients except salmon and chill 8 hours. Add salmon and serve with crackers.

1 package frozen chopped spinach, thawed and drained
1 package dry gourmet vegetable soup mix
2 cups sour cream
1 cup mayonnaise
1 8-ounce can water chestnuts, chopped
2 cups cooked flaked salmon

Cottage Cheese and Salmon Dip

Combine mayonnaise and salmon. Mix well with fork. Add cottage cheese, salt and pepper. Chill. Serve with crackers or toast rounds.

2 cups salmon, cooked and finely flaked
1 cup mayonnaise
1½ cups small curd cottage cheese
salt and white pepper to taste

Salmon Quiche Spread

Combine all ingredients. Place in quiche dish and bake at 350° for 15 minutes. Serve with crackers.

2 8-ounce packages cream cheese
4 tablespoons chopped onion
4 tablespoons milk
1 cup smoked salmon, finely flaked
4 tablespoons chopped green pepper
1 cup sour cream
1 cup chopped walnuts

Irene's Salmon Spread

Place cream cheese and soup in saucepan. Heat over low heat until cheese melts.

Mix gelatin with 1 tablespoon boiling water until dissolved. Add to cheese mixture. Remove from heat and add remaining ingredients.

Pour into mold. Refrigerate overnight. Serve with crackers.

2 3-ounce packages cream cheese
1 can mushroom soup
1 envelope gelatin
1 cup finely chopped celery
1 cup mayonnaise
3 green onions, finely chopped
2 cups cooked salmon, flaked

Easy Salmon Dip

Combine ingredients. Chill before serving. Serve with chips or crackers.

To vary, substitute 8 ounces softened cream cheese in place of sour cream.

1 cup sour cream
2 cups smoked salmon, crumbled
garlic salt to taste
salt and pepper to taste

Salmon Mousse

Heat vermouth and gelatin in saucepan. Remove from heat and let stand 10 minutes.

Meanwhile, combine remaining ingredients until well blended. Stir in gelatin mixture and pour into a 2-cup flat bottom mold.

Chill at least 3 hours or overnight.

Remove from mold. Serve with crackers.

½ cup dry vermouth
1 envelope unflavored gelatin
1 cup smoked salmon, flaked
3 hard-cooked eggs, mashed
¾ cup sour cream
½ cup sliced green onions
¼ cup parsley
3 tablespoons mayonnaise
1 teaspoon prepared horseradish

Salmon Artichoke Tidbits

Mix all ingredients thoroughly. Place in a buttered 9-inch baking pan. Bake at 325° for 1 hour. Cut into 32 tidbits.

1 cup smoked salmon, finely flaked

4 eggs

½ pound cheddar cheese, grated

2 6-ounce cans marinated artichoke hearts, drained and chopped

3 green onions, finely chopped

12 saltine crackers, crushed

SOUPS &
BREADS

Neah Bay Chowder

Clean and wash squid. In a saucepan, cover squid with 1/2 gallon milk and bring to a near boil. Do not scald milk. Milk should turn slightly pink. Remove from heat and drain, reserving liquid. Immediately rinse squid with cold water.

In a large soup pot measure 1 1/2 quarts reserved liquid. Stir in sour cream, cheese, salt, pepper and wine and stir well. Then add chicken, 2 cups chopped squid, scallops, clams, shrimp, salmon and parsley. Dissolve arrowroot in 3 tablespoons of water and add to soup. Simmer very slowly for 10 minutes stirring occasionally to thicken soup.

Serves 8.

3 pounds squid
1/2 gallon milk
1 cup sour cream
2 cups shredded sharp cheddar cheese
2 teaspoons salt
1/2 teaspoon white pepper
1/4 cup Madeira wine
1/4 cup diced raw chicken breast, skinned
1 cup cubed scallops (1/2-inch cubes)
1 cup whole baby clams, drained
1 cup small salad shrimp
1 cup cubed raw salmon (1-inch cubes)
1 cup finely chopped fresh parsley
3 tablespoons arrowroot

Tureen à Salmon

Thaw pastry dough for 20 minutes; unfold sheets. Roll dough on lightly floured board to remove creases. Using soup tureen as guide, cut pastry in circles 1 inch larger than the tureen.

Combine remaining ingredients in a saucepan and heat, do not boil. Place in individual tureens and cover with puff pastry. Bake in a 400° oven until puffed and brown. Serve immediately.

Serves 4.

1 package frozen puff pastry
1/4 cup thinly sliced carrots
4 cups chicken broth
1 cup chopped celery
1/4 cup chopped green onion
    pinch of tarragon
1/4 cup sliced water chestnuts
1 1/2 cups uncooked salmon, cut into bite-size pieces
    salt and pepper to taste
4 ovenproof soup tureens

Shilshole Bay Chowder

In a skillet fry bacon until crisp, remove. Sauté onion in bacon fat.

Transfer contents of skillet to a saucepan and stir in flour until smooth. Add potatoes, water, salt, pepper and dill. Bring to a boil, cover, reduce heat and simmer for about 10 minutes or until potatoes are tender.

Add salmon, cover and simmer approximately 10 minutes until salmon is tender. Add remaining ingredients and heat but do not boil. Sprinkle with crumbled bacon and parsley.

Serves 6.

1 pound salmon fillet, skinned and cut into 1-inch chunks
4 slices bacon
1 onion, chopped
1 tablespoon flour
2 potatoes, peeled and diced
1 cup water
1/8 teaspoon dill
1 8-ounce can whole kernel corn, undrained
1 cup milk
1 cup half-and-half
salt and pepper to taste
chopped parsley to garnish

Salmon Soup Extraordinaire

Cover salmon with cold water and salt and let stand 1 hour.

Drain and rinse fish. Place in soup pot with remaining ingredients except almond extract. Bring to a boil, cover and gently simmer for 40 minutes. Remove from heat and let stand 10 minutes.

Add almond extract and serve immediately.

Serves 6 to 8.

2½ cups uncooked salmon, broken into bite-size pieces
    cold water
  2 teaspoons salt
  1 20-ounce can whole tomatoes
  ½ cup chopped onion
  4 whole bay leaves
  2 cups chopped celery
  1 teaspoon black pepper
  ½ teaspoon almond extract

Ron's Bisque

Cook salmon over medium heat for 2 to 3 minutes in chicken broth. Set aside until cool.

Pour water into blender. Add salmon, onion, reserved chicken bouillon, flour and milk. Blend on high speed for 1 minute.

Pour mixture into top of double boiler and cook over simmering water for 30 minutes. Stir occasionally. Add cream, sherry and butter. Stir until butter dissolves. Add salt, pepper and dash of cayenne pepper to taste.

Serves 2.

2 cups salmon, skinned, boned and cubed
1/2 cup cold water
8 ounces chicken bouillon
2 tablespoons onion, diced
2 tablespoons flour
3/4 cup milk
1/4 cup light cream
2 tablespoons dry sherry
2 tablespoons butter
salt
pepper
cayenne pepper

East Bay Chowder

In a saucepan bring broth to a boil. Add
diced potato. Cover and simmer until
potato is tender, about 5 to 8 minutes.

Add butter. Slowly stir in instant potato
and continue to stir until smooth. Add
half-and-half and tarragon and simmer
3 to 4 minutes.

Just before serving, add salmon, chives
and pepper.

Serves 4.

2 cups chicken broth
1 medium potato, diced
1 tablespoon butter
1/3 cup instant mashed
    potato
1/2 cup half-and-half or
    light cream
    pinch of tarragon
1 cup cooked salmon
1 teaspoon chopped
    chives
    fresh ground pepper
    to taste

Glacier Bear Beer Bread

Preheat oven to 375°.

Sift together flour and sugar. Blend cheese squares, onion, and salmon with flour mixture. Add beer and mix thoroughly. Batter will be thick.

Liberally grease 2 regular and 1 small bread pans or 5 small loaf pans. Fill pans ½ full and let stand 10 minutes. Bake 50 to 55 minutes or until golden brown. Remove from oven and brush tops with melted butter. Remove immediately from pans. Serve bread warm with butter.

Bread may be reheated by wrapping in foil and placing in a 350° oven. Do not use a microwave.

For a special treat, slice the leftover bread, toast, and spread with cream cheese.

6 cups self-rising flour
1 cup sugar
12 ounces mild cheddar cheese cut into ¼-inch squares
⅓ cup dried minced onion
1 cup finely flaked smoked salmon
2 cans light beer

Smoked Salmon, Olive and Cheddar Bread

Mix flour, sugar, baking powder, baking soda, salt and cayenne. Cut in butter with fork. Add cheese.

In a separate bowl, combine egg, buttermilk and Worcestershire. Add to flour mixture and mix just until moistened. Add salmon and olives.

Place batter in greased bread pan (8½ × 4½ × 2½). Bake at 375° for 1 hour or until golden brown.

2½ cups flour
2½ tablespoons sugar
2 teaspoons baking powder
½ teaspoon baking soda
1 teaspoon salt
⅛ teaspoon cayenne
¼ cup butter
1 cup shredded sharp cheddar cheese
1 egg
1 cup buttermilk
1 teaspoon Worcestershire sauce
1 cup black olives, coarsely chopped
1 cup smoked salmon, shredded (food processor with metal blade works great)

Jerrilynn's Smoked Salmon Sourdough

Combine sourdough starter, water, 3 cups flour and salt. Gradually add the rest of the flour to make a stiff dough. Turn out on a kneading board, working in flour and air until dough springs back from poking with finger. Place in a bowl, cover and let rise 2 to 4 hours until double in size.

Shape into 2 large loaves or 3 medium loaves. Make a lengthwise cut down the middle and halfway through each loaf. Add equal amounts of onion, salmon and cheese to each loaf. Roll loaves to completely cover salmon centers and let rise 30 to 40 minutes on a baking sheet sprinkled with cornmeal. Place in 400° oven. After 15 minutes, reduce heat to 350° and bake for another 20 minutes or until golden brown.

The cornmeal on the baking sheet will add flavor, prevent burning and eliminate oil in the baking process.

3 cups sourdough starter
2 cups water
9 cups unbleached white flour
2 teaspoons salt
1 heaping teaspoon gluten (optional)
1 cup smoked salmon, flaked
1 small onion, chopped fine
1 cup cheddar cheese, grated
cornmeal

SALADS

Salmon and Lettuce Toss

Break up lettuce into a chilled salad
bowl. Toss with salmon and bacon bits.
Sprinkle with parmesan. Toss lightly
with dressing.

romaine lettuce
red leaf lettuce
bibb lettuce
chunks of cold cooked
salmon (1/4 cup per
person)
bacon bits
grated parmesan
cheese
Italian dressing

Salmon Overnighter

Arrange layer of lettuce in bowl.
Continue to layer each of the following:
green onions, white radishes, water
chestnuts, green pepper and frozen
peas. Spread mayonnaise over peas.
Sprinkle with sugar, parmesan and salt.
Cover with smoked salmon and then a
layer of eggs. Cover bowl and chill
overnight. Serve with tomato wedges on
top of salad.

1 head iceberg lettuce, shredded
8 green onions, sliced
8 white radishes, sliced
1 8-ounce can water chestnuts, sliced
1 green pepper, seeded and sliced
1 package frozen peas
2 cups mayonnaise
3 teaspoons sugar
1 cup grated parmesan cheese
1 teaspoon salt
1 cup smoked salmon, flaked
3 hard-boiled eggs, shredded
2 tomatoes, wedged

Salmon Waldorf

Sprinkle lemon juice over apples. Toss with remaining ingredients. Serve in lettuce cups with Honey Lime Dressing.

1 cup cooked salmon, cut into bite-size pieces
1 tablespoon lemon juice
1 cup diced apple
1 cup chopped celery
½ cup salted nuts (walnuts)
Honey Lime Dressing (below)

Honey Lime Dressing

1 part lime juice to 2 parts honey. Shake ingredients well in a tightly covered jar.

limes
honey

Salmon and Cucumber Toss

Toss ingredients together. Generously coat with creamy cucumber or honey mustard dressing.

1 cup chopped lettuce (per serving)

¼ cucumber, peeled and chopped (per serving)

¼ cup cooked cold salmon, poached or barbecued (per serving)

Salmon Louis

Arrange lettuce in bowl. Place salmon on lettuce. Garnish with tomatoes, cucumbers and hard-boiled eggs.

Excellent with leftover barbecued salmon.

iceberg lettuce, shredded
salmon, cooked and chunked (¾ cup per person)
tomatoes, wedged
cucumbers, sliced
hard-boiled eggs, sliced
Dressing (below)

Dressing

Combine dressing ingredients and chill for several hours.

2 cups mayonnaise
juice of ½ lemon
½ cup chili sauce
½ cup chopped onion
½ cup chopped green pepper
½ teaspoon paprika
salt and pepper to taste

Duncan's Anchovy-Salmon Salad

Break lettuce into bite-size pieces in salad bowl. Cover with salmon, beans, eggs, tomatoes, and onions. Toss gently with dressing. Garnish with olives and anchovies.

Serves 6.

½ head lettuce
2 cups cooked salmon, chunked
1 16-ounce can green beans, drained
2 hard-boiled eggs, quartered
12 cherry tomatoes, cut in half
1 red onion, thinly sliced and separated into rings
Italian dressing
½ cup pitted ripe olives
1 2-ounce can anchovy fillets, drained

Salmon Niçoise

Slice 1½ potatoes on each of 6 chilled salad plates. Spread green pepper, tomatoes, onions and salmon on top of potatoes. Add desired amount of dressing and garnish with black olives.

Serves 6.

9 red unpeeled potatoes, cooked and chilled
2 small green peppers, chopped
2 tomatoes, chopped
2 small onions, thinly sliced and separated into rings
2 cups cooked salmon, flaked
   creamy cucumber dressing
   black olives

VEGETABLES

Onions Stuffed With Mushrooms and Salmon

Cut top off one end of each onion and remove first layer. Blanch onions for 4 to 5 minutes. Drain and cool. Cut off other end of each onion and remove center.

Cook mushrooms in butter until tender. Remove from heat. Blend in flour, salt and dill. Stir in half-and-half and cook until thickened. Add peas and salmon.

Fill onion shells. Place in a buttered baking dish and bake at 375° for 20 minutes.

Serves 6.

6 onions (preferably Walla Walla Sweets)
2 cups sliced fresh mushrooms
2 tablespoons butter
1 tablespoon flour
1 teaspoon salt
½ teaspoon dill
½ cup half-and-half
1 cup frozen green peas, cooked
1 cup cooked salmon, flaked

Salmon Stuffed Green Peppers

Cut the stem end off the green peppers and remove membrane and seeds. Parboil peppers for 10 minutes and drain.

Combine the remaining ingredients except the cheddar cheese. Mix well. Stuff each pepper and place in a greased baking dish.

Bake in a 350° oven for 20 minutes. Remove from oven and sprinkle tops with cheddar cheese. Return to oven for 10 minutes.

Serves 6.

6	large green peppers
1½	cups cooked salmon, flaked
2	cups cooked rice
½	cup onion, chopped fine
1	8-ounce can tomato sauce
1	egg, well beaten
1	tablespoon lemon juice
1	teaspoon salt
½	teaspoon white pepper
1	teaspoon dill
1½	cups cheddar cheese, grated

Salmon Stuffed Cabbage

Blanch cabbage leaves. Meanwhile, cook sausage and break into fine pieces. Drain fat and add salmon, green onions, rice, salt and pepper. Mix thoroughly.

Take large cabbage leaf and place 3 tablespoons stuffing at one end. Roll once, fold in corners, continue to roll and fasten with toothpicks. Place in large skillet. Add tomatoes and juice, cover and simmer 30 minutes.

Ladle sauce on serving platter. Place cabbage rolls on sauce and serve immediately.

Serves 6.

1 head cabbage
1 pound pork sausage
2½ cups cooked salmon, broken into bite-size pieces
1 bunch green onions, sliced thinly
3 cups cooked rice
   salt to taste
   white pepper to taste
1 28-ounce can whole tomatoes, chopped

Salmon Stuffed Potatoes

Scrub potatoes and rub with vegetable oil. Bake in a 450° oven until tender.

Slice potatoes in half lengthwise and scoop out inside of potato leaving a thin shell. Discard 4 of the shells.

Add remaining ingredients to potato pulp and mash with a fork (do not use a beater). Fill 8 potato skins and sprinkle with paprika.

Return to a 350° oven for 20 minutes. Place under broiler the last 2 minutes or until golden brown.

Serves 8.

6 potatoes
1 cup grated cheddar cheese
1/4 cup chopped green onion
4 tablespoons butter
8 ounces sour cream
1 cup finely flaked smoked salmon
  salt and pepper to taste
  paprika

Salmon Stuffed Zucchini

Cut off ends of zucchini. Heat 1 inch of salted water to boiling. Add whole unpared zucchini; cover and heat to boiling. Reduce heat; simmer until tender, 12 to 15 minutes. Drain; cool slightly.

In a small saucepan cook onion in butter until tender. In a large bowl combine rice, sour cream, bay leaf, salt, pepper, green chilies, onion and salmon.

Cut each zucchini lengthwise in half. Carefully scoop out pulp leaving a ¼-inch shell. Fill each shell with salmon mixture. Place in a buttered baking dish.

Bake in a 350° oven for 10 minutes. Remove from oven and sprinkle cheddar cheese on top of each zucchini. Bake an additional 10 minutes.

Serves 8.

4 medium zucchini
1 cup chopped onion
¼ cup butter
1½ cups cooked rice
1½ cups sour cream
1 bay leaf, crushed
½ teaspoon salt
½ teaspoon pepper
2 4-ounce cans whole green chili peppers, chopped
1½ cups cooked salmon, flaked
1½ cups shredded cheddar cheese

Salmon Stuffed Mushrooms

Scrub mushrooms. Remove centers and discard.

Combine remaining ingredients in a mixing bowl. Stuff mushrooms.

Place on a buttered cookie sheet. Bake in a 350° oven for about 20 minutes.

Serves 6.

24 large mushrooms
1 cup salmon, cooked and flaked
1 egg, beaten
2 slices bread, crumbled
1/4 cup thinly sliced green onion
1/4 cup finely chopped celery
1/2 teaspoon ground nutmeg
1/4 teaspoon salt
1/4 teaspoon pepper

Salmon Stuffed Tomatoes

Cut tops off tomatoes. Remove centers, leaving shells. Invert to drain.

Sauté garlic in butter until lightly browned. Remove from heat. Stir in cooked rice, 1 cup cheddar cheese, mushrooms, milk, parsley, salt, basil and salmon.

Lightly salt inside of tomato shells. Fill with rice mixture. Bake in a 375° oven 10 minutes. Remove and sprinkle with remaining cheddar cheese. Bake an additional 10 minutes.

Serves 6.

6 tomatoes
1 clove garlic, minced
1 tablespoon butter
1 cup cooked rice
2 cups cheddar cheese, grated
1 4-ounce can chopped mushrooms, drained
4 tablespoons milk
1 tablespoon parsley
1 teaspoon salt
1 teaspoon basil, crushed
1½ cups cooked salmon, flaked

PASTA

Salmonghetti

Lightly brown bacon in skillet. Remove and cut each slice into 3 pieces. Reserve 2 tablespoons bacon grease and sauté onions and mushrooms. Add olives, tomatoes with their juice, tomato sauce and bacon and simmer 30 minutes.

Cook fettucini or spaghetti according to directions on package. Drain.

Add salmon to tomato mixture.

In a buttered casserole dish, place a layer of pasta, ½ the sauce and 2 cups cheese. Repeat.

Bake at 350° for 20 minutes.

Serves 12.

10 slices bacon
2 tablespoons bacon grease
2 onions, sliced
½ pound mushrooms, sliced
1 cup black olives, sliced
1 28-ounce can whole tomatoes
1 8-ounce can tomato sauce
1 12-ounce package long egg fettucini or spaghetti, cooked
3 cups cooked salmon, flaked
4 cups shredded medium cheddar cheese

Salmon Pastitsio

Cook macaroni according to package instructions. Drain and cool to lukewarm. Mix with beaten egg.

In a large skillet melt butter and cook onion until tender. Add tomato puree, tomato paste, pepper and cinnamon. Salt to taste. Cover and simmer for about 20 minutes. Add bread crumbs and salmon. Cover and simmer for 10 minutes longer.

In a 13½ × 8¾ × 1¾ dish place half of the macaroni and sprinkle with ¼ cup parmesan and ¼ cup romano. Spread salmon mixture on top and sprinkle with ¼ cup parmesan and ¼ cup romano cheese. Add the remaining macaroni. Pour the egg sauce over the top and let it run down the edges. Sprinkle with remaining cheese.

Bake at 375° for 30 to 40 minutes. Cheese should bubble and brown on top. Let sit for about 10 minutes before slicing.

Serves 8.

4	cups elbow macaroni
1	egg
2	tablespoons butter
1	onion, chopped
4	cups cooked salmon, broken into bite-size pieces
1¼	cups tomato puree
1	cup tomato paste
¼	teaspoon pepper
¼	teaspoon cinnamon
½	cup dry bread crumbs
1½	cups freshly grated romano cheese
1½	cups freshly grated parmesan
	Egg Sauce (below)

Egg Sauce

Melt butter in pan on medium heat. Add flour, salt, pepper and nutmeg. Gradually stir in 2½ cups milk. Cook over medium heat until thickened and boiling. Add beaten eggs to remaining ½ cup milk and stir into sauce. Cook a minute or so longer.

⅓	cup butter
⅓	cup flour
1½	teaspoons salt
¼	teaspoon white pepper
¼	teaspoon nutmeg
3	cups milk
2	eggs

Easy Salmon Pasta

Cook pasta according to directions. Meanwhile wrap salmon in foil and heat in warm oven.

Melt butter in saucepan. Add cream and simmer for 5 minutes. Add scotch. Pour over cooked pasta. Sprinkle with capers, smoked salmon and nutmeg.

Serves 4 to 6.

pasta (fettucini is wonderful)
1/4 pound butter
2 cups whipping cream
1/2 ounce scotch
1 tablespoon capers
smoked salmon (1/4 cup per person)
freshly ground nutmeg

Salmon Tetrazzini

Cook spaghetti and set aside.

Sauté onion in butter. Add ½ cup cheese and remaining ingredients. Combine with spaghetti and place in a buttered casserole dish. Top with remaining cheese. Heat under broiler until cheese is golden brown.

Serves 6.

8 ounces spaghetti, cooked
½ cup chopped onion
2 tablespoons butter
1 cup grated romano cheese
2 cans cream of mushroom soup
1 cup water
1 8-ounce can mushrooms, stems and pieces
3 cups salmon, cooked and broken into small chunks
2 tablespoons parsley
2 teaspoons lemon juice
⅛ teaspoon thyme
⅛ teaspoon marjoram

Salmon Marinara

Sauté garlic until brown in olive oil. Add green onions and celery. Sieve tomatoes and add both tomatoes and reserved juice to onions and celery. Add remaining 4 ingredients except salmon and simmer 30 to 40 minutes. Add salmon the last 10 minutes. Serve over spaghetti.

Serves 4.

3 garlic cloves, finely chopped
3 tablespoons olive oil
1/3 cup chopped green onions (use the whole onion)
1/3 cup finely chopped celery
1 28-ounce can whole peeled tomatoes; reserve juice
2 tablespoons oregano
juice of 1/2 lemon
salt and white pepper to taste
1 6-ounce can tomato paste
3 cups uncooked skinned salmon fillets, cut in 1-inch pieces

Salmon Fettucini

Melt butter in a saucepan. Add flour stirring constantly. Add half-and-half and chicken broth. Bring to a boil while continuing to stir. Remove from heat. Add Madeira, salt, pepper, nutmeg and vinegar; stir until blended. Place in top of double boiler and keep warm on stove.

Cook fettucini according to directions on package except add rice wine vinegar to boiling water. Drain and rinse in hot water.

Arrange fettucini on 4 heated dinner plates. Lightly toss each serving with 1/3 cup of smoked salmon. Ladle sauce over the top.

Serves 4.

- 6 tablespoons butter
- 6 tablespoons flour
- 2 1/2 cups half-and-half
- 1/2 cup chicken broth
- 4 tablespoons Madeira
- 3/4 teaspoon salt
- 3/4 teaspoon white pepper
- 3/4 teaspoon nutmeg
- 1 1/2 teaspoons rice wine vinegar
- 4 cups uncooked fettucini noodles
- 1 1/3 cups flaked smoked salmon

Salmon Manicotti

Cook manicotti shells according to package directions. Do not over cook.

In a bowl mix remaining ingredients except tomato sauce. Stuff shells with mixture. Pour about ¾ of the tomato sauce over the bottom of a large pan and place shells on top. Spread the remaining sauce over the top of the shells to keep moist.

Bake at 350° about 20 minutes or until sauce is bubbly and cheese is melted. If desired, sprinkle more cheese on the top while baking.

Serves 4.

8   manicotti shells
2   cups cooked flaked salmon (poached, barbecued, or broiled)
1   cup grated cheddar cheese
1   cup grated mozzarella cheese
1   teaspoon lemon juice
6   tablespoons sour cream
2   onions finely chopped
10 ounces tomato sauce

Pav's Pasta

Generously season each fillet with lemon juice, salt and pepper. Set aside.

Roll pasta sheet slightly larger than fillet and approximately ⅛-inch thick. Place 1 fillet on each sheet and roll in jelly roll fashion. Moisten and seal edges and ends.

Place in a large pan of boiling salt water for 20-30 minutes or until pasta is cooked. Turn pasta in pan 3 or 4 times during cooking. While pasta is cooking, melt butter in medium pan. Add cream and bring to a low boil. Remove from heat and add the Worcestershire sauce.

Slice pasta and serve with warm cream sauce.

Serves 4-6.

* Prepare your homemade pasta or use commercial pasta, available at gourmet shops or in the frozen food section at your supermarket.

2 sheets spinach pasta*
2 salmon fillets, boned and skinned
   lemon juice
   salt
   pepper
10 tablespoons butter
1½ cups cream
8 tablespoons Worcestershire sauce

ENTREES

Capilano Salmon Ring

Mix together all ingredients. Place in a buttered ring mold. Bake in a 350° oven for 40 to 50 minutes until lightly browned on top. Unmold on serving platter garnished with lettuce. Fill center of ring with steamed rice or fresh green peas. Serve with Hollandaise Sauce (see page 155).

* Basic White Sauce, see page 156.

3 cups cooked flaked salmon
1 tablespoon grated onion
1/4 cup chopped stuffed olives
1 tablespoon dried parsley
1 teaspoon salt
   dash of pepper
1 tablespoon lemon juice
2 eggs slightly beaten
3/4 cup Basic White Sauce*

Salmon Neptune

Cook noodles according to directions on package. Drain.

In skillet sauté onions, carrots, parsley, and dill in oil until tender. In a greased baking dish combine flaked salmon, vegetables and noodles. Add milk, salt and pepper. Sprinkle cheese over the top. Bake at 350° until the cheese melts.

Serves 6.

3 cups extra wide egg noodles
2 onions, chopped
3 carrots, thinly sliced
3 tablespoons dried parsley
1 teaspoon dill
3 tablespoons oil
1 cup cooked salmon, flaked
1/2 cup milk
salt and pepper to taste
3 cups grated cheddar cheese

Salmon and Shrimp Stroganoff

Sauté onions and mushrooms in butter until tender. Add tomatoes (with juice), salt, pepper, Worcestershire, lime juice, ketchup and nutmeg.

Simmer uncovered for about 10 minutes stirring frequently. Add shrimp and salmon, and simmer for 2 to 3 minutes longer.

Blend together sour cream and flour. Slowly add to salmon mixture. Cook stirring constantly for 1 minute. Serve over egg noodles.

Serves 6.

1	onion, sliced thin
1/2	pound mushrooms, thinly sliced
1/4	cup butter
1	16-ounce can tomatoes, chopped
1/2	teaspoon salt
1/4	teaspoon pepper
1	teaspoon Worcestershire sauce
1	tablespoon lime juice
1	tablespoon ketchup dash nutmeg
20	medium size raw shrimp, shelled and deveined
1	cup uncooked salmon fillets, skinned and cut into 1 1/2 inch pieces
1	cup sour cream
2	tablespoons flour

Sholley's Salmon Loaf

Sprinkle salmon with lemon juice, paprika, and onion salt. Combine salmon with wheat germ, whole wheat cracker crumbs, celery, and green pepper. Add milk and eggs. Pack into a greased loaf pan.

Bake at 325° for 1¼ to 1½ hours. Loaf will be firm and brown.

Serves 4 to 6.

1½ cups cooked flaked salmon
juice of ½ lemon
⅛ teaspoon paprika
¼ teaspoon onion salt
½ cup wheat germ
½ cup cracked wheat bulgur
½ cup chopped celery
¼ cup minced green pepper
1 cup milk
2 eggs, beaten

Beau Chené Stuffed Shrimp

Shell and devein shrimp leaving the last shell and tail intact. Butterfly shrimp. (Do not cut completely through shrimp.) Set aside.

Combine salmon, green onion, salt and pepper to taste.

Separate each egg roll wrapper and place on a dry surface. Place slice of ham on each egg roll wrapper. Place a shrimp on top of each slice of ham. Place salmon stuffing on top of each shrimp.

Wrap ham around salmon-stuffed shrimp leaving last shell and tail exposed. Fold egg roll around each ham-wrapped shrimp, again leaving last shell and tail exposed. Seal edges by moistening with water.

Heat vegetable shortening until hot in wok or deep fryer. Fry 2 to 3 shrimp at a time, turning to cook evenly until golden brown. Remove and drain.

Serve with your favorite sweet-and-sour sauce.

Serves 8.

8 large shrimp, 8- to 10-count size
2 cups cooked salmon, flaked
1 whole green onion, minced
  salt and pepper to taste
  vegetable shortening
8 egg roll wrappers
8 slices ham, paper thin

Salmon Stuffed Squid

Clean and wash squid. In a saucepan, cover squid with milk and bring to a near boil. Do not scald milk. Drain immediately and run squid under cold water.

Stuffing

Cut ¼ inch off of the open end of each squid. Chop ends into small pieces until you have 1 cup. Mix with green onion tops, bread crumbs, eggs, poached salmon, coriander, pepper, salt and ¼ cup melted butter.

Stuff each squid to within ½ inch from top. Seal in stuffing with a whole cherry at the end and secure with a toothpick. Place squid side by side in a buttered baking dish. Chop remaining cherries and add reserved juice. Place in a saucepan and bring to a boil. Pour over squid. Bake covered at 375° for 20 to 30 minutes. Sauce may be served over squid or on the side.

14 squid
1 quart milk
1 cup finely chopped green onion tops
1 cup Italian-style bread crumbs
2 eggs
2 cups lightly poached salmon, broken into pieces
½ teaspoon ground coriander
½ teaspoon white pepper
½ teaspoon salt
½ cup butter
1 cup chopped green onion
1 8¾-ounce can dark sweet pitted cherries, reserve juice

Mustard Honey Barbecue

In a small saucepan combine honey, mustard, lemon juice, butter and coriander. Cook over medium heat until butter melts. Stir until smooth. Set aside.

Place salmon on barbecue flesh side down long enough to give meat color. Turn over to skin side down. Brush with marinade several times while salmon is cooking. Continue to barbecue until fish flakes easily with a fork.

This salmon is excellent served cold.

1 cup honey
1 tablespoon mustard
1 tablespoon lemon juice
4 tablespoons butter
1 teaspoon coriander
  salmon fillet

Poached Salmon

Place fish in a foil lined pan skin-side down. (Pan should be large enough to hold fish with an inch around each side.) Sprinkle with salt, pepper and tarragon. Place thinly sliced lemons over top of fish. Barely cover fish with milk.

Bake covered with foil in a 350° oven until fish flakes easily when tested with a fork.

Remove fish to platter. Measure 2 cups of poaching liquid in a small saucepan. Add 1 cup of milk to liquid. Dissolve arrowroot in 2 tablespoons water. Add to milk mixture and cook over medium heat until thickened. Add mustard and stir until well blended. Serve over fish.

Serves 6 to 8.

2-4 pounds of salmon fillets
salt and pepper
1½ teaspoons crushed tarragon
lemon slices
1 cup milk
2 tablespoons arrowroot
1 tablespoon mustard

Salmon Newburg

In a large skillet melt butter and sauté onion until tender. Add Madeira and nutmeg. Combine cream and egg yolks in a bowl and slowly add to skillet stirring constantly. Continue to stir until sauce thickens. Fold in salmon and heat 1 minute.

Serve at once over rice.

Serves 4.

1 cup butter
1 tablespoon chopped onion
½ cup Madeira
½ teaspoon nutmeg
2 cups cream
6 egg yolks
1½ cups cooked chunked salmon, broiled or poached

Salmon Soufflé

Dice 4 slices of the bread in soufflé dish. Mix together salmon, mayonnaise, onion, green pepper and celery and spread over bread. Trim crust from rest of bread and place bread on top of the salmon mixture. Mix eggs and milk together and pour over bread. Keep in refrigerator overnight.

Bake in a 325° oven for 15 minutes. Remove from oven and pour the mushroom soup over the top. Cover with cheddar cheese and sprinkle with paprika. Bake 1 hour longer.

Serves 10.

8 slices white bread
4 cups cooked salmon, cut into bite-size pieces
1/2 cup mayonnaise
1 chopped onion
1 chopped green pepper
1 cup finely chopped celery
4 eggs
3 cups milk
1 can mushroom soup
2 cups grated medium cheddar cheese
    paprika

Salmon Enchiladas

Sauté onion and garlic in oil. Add tomato puree, green chilies, salmon and salt. Simmer 5 minutes.

In a 1-quart saucepan, dissolve bouillon cubes in ¼ cup boiling water. Add half-and-half and heat.

Fry 1 dozen tortillas in 1 inch hot oil. Do not let them become crisp. Dip each tortilla into half-and-half mixture. Add salmon filling and roll up.

In a large baking dish pour ½ of the half-and-half, then arrange rolls in dish. Cover with remaining half-and-half. Bake in 350° oven for 15 minutes. Top with cheese and bake 15 minutes longer.

Serves 6.

1 onion, chopped
1 clove of garlic, crushed
2 tablespoons vegetable oil
2 cups tomato puree
2 canned green chilies, chopped
2 cups cooked salmon, chopped into chunks
1 teaspoon salt
6 chicken bouillon cubes
¼ cup water
3 cups half-and-half
1 dozen medium flour tortillas
1 pound grated monterey jack cheese

Court Bouillon

Sauté vegetables in butter until tender. Add remaining ingredients except salmon in a large pan and bring to a boil. Reduce heat and simmer bouillon 5 minutes.

Place fish in a foil lined pan. Cover with bouillon. Bake covered with foil in a 350° oven until fish flakes easily when tested with a fork.

For variation: Follow above directions except omit cloves and lemon juice and replace with ½ teaspoon ginger and ¼ cup vinegar.

½ cup sliced onion
½ cup diced carrots
2 tablespoons diced green pepper
½ cup chopped celery
2 tablespoons butter
2-3 whole cloves
2 teaspoons salt
4-5 peppercorns
1 bay leaf
½ cup lemon juice
2½ quarts water
salmon fillets, skinned (up to 4 pounds)

Salmon Turnovers

Combine all ingredients except pastry dough and let stand 1 hour in the refrigerator.

Remove puff pastry dough from freezer, let thaw and roll out into 5-inch squares. Place a heaping tablespoon of salmon mixture in the center. Fold over, forming a triangle and seal with a fork. Bake in a 400° oven until puffed and golden brown.

For a glazed effect, brush with slightly beaten egg white.

*Basic White Sauce, see page 156.

1 cup flaked poached salmon
1 teaspoon grated onion
1 tablespoon finely minced sweet pickle
2 teaspoons lemon juice
3/4 cup Basic White Sauce
frozen puff pastry dough

Classic Salmon Loaf

Mix together all ingredients.

Pack into a greased loaf pan and bake at 375° for 30 to 45 minutes until firm and brown.

Serves 4 to 6.

1/2	cup fine dry bread or cracker crumbs
2 1/2	cups cooked flaked salmon
1/3	cup chopped green onion
1/2	cup finely chopped celery
	juice of 1/2 lemon
1	teaspoon salt
1/2	teaspoon pepper
1	large egg or 2 medium eggs
1/2	cup mayonnaise

Salmon Curry

Sauté onion and green pepper in butter until tender. Blend in flour. Stir in half-and-half, then remaining ingredients except salmon. Cook until thickened. Add salmon and cook over low heat for approximately 10 minutes.

Serve over white rice with your favorite condiments.

Serves 4.

1 onion, chopped
1 green pepper, chopped
4 tablespoons butter
3 tablespoons flour
2 cups half-and-half
1 clove garlic, mashed
1½ teaspoons curry powder
1 tablespoon lemon juice
½ teaspoon salt
½ teaspoon ground ginger
⅛ teaspoon pepper
⅛ teaspoon chili powder
1 small salmon fillet, skinned and cut into 1-inch pieces

Tolovana Cioppino

In a giant saucepan sauté onions, green peppers and garlic in olive oil about 5 minutes. Add all ingredients except wine and seafood.

Cover and simmer 1 hour. Stir in wine and simmer 30 minutes longer. Add clams and crab; be sure to separate the legs from the body and break each leg before adding to pan. (Tap each leg on board with a hammer.) Add the remaining seafood.

Cover and simmer until the clam shells open. Add remaining seafood and simmer approximately 10 minutes or until fish is done.

Serve with green salad and lots of garlic bread.

Serves 14.

3 onions, chopped
3 green peppers, chopped
4 cloves garlic, chopped finely
3/4 cup olive oil
3 28-ounce cans whole tomatoes, cut in quarters
3/4 cup parsley
1/4 cup rosemary
2 tablespoons sage
2 tablespoons thyme
4 tablespoons basil
1/4 cup marjoram
1 6-ounce can tomato paste
1 quart clamato juice
1 tablespoon white pepper
1 bunch spinach, coarsely cut
1 15-ounce can tomato sauce
2 cups water
2 cups white or red wine
3 dozen steamer clams, scrubbed well
3 dozen prawns, shelled and deveined
4 Dungeness crabs, cracked and cleaned
2 pounds halibut, cut into 1-inch pieces and skinned
2 pounds salmon, cut into 1-inch pieces and skinned
1 pound scallops

Salmon Shish Kabobs

Prepare Teriyaki Sauce according to directions on page 149. Cool. Alternate salmon, zucchini, onion, tomatoes and mushrooms on skewers.

Marinate in Teriyaki Sauce in refrigerator for 4 hours.

Place skewers on barbecue for 10 to 15 minutes or until fish is done. Turn 2 to 3 times while cooking. Serve over hot cooked rice.

Serves 4.

1 salmon fillet, skinned and cut into 2-inch squares
1 medium zucchini, cut into 12 slices 1/4 inch thick
1 onion, cut into 12 pieces
12 cherry tomatoes
12 mushroom caps
   Teriyaki Sauce
4 servings hot cooked rice
4 skewers, well greased

Salmon Ronaldo

Preheat oven to 375°. Pound chicken breast flat and marinate in orange juice for 2 to 3 hours.

Prepare stuffing: Mix together salmon, lemon juice, pepper, dill, ½ cup crushed cheese crackers, onion, and ½ cup melted butter.

Divide stuffing equally and place on top of each chicken breast. Roll breast and secure with a toothpick, sealing ends well. Dip chicken breasts in orange juice and roll in remaining cracker crumbs. Melt remaining ½ cup butter in skillet and place chicken rolls in skillet. Brown, turning until well sealed, approximately 2 minutes. Remove and place chicken breasts in a greased baking pan.

Place the remaining crackers and 1 cup of orange juice in the skillet that the chicken rolls were browned in and stir over medium heat until thickened. Pour over the chicken. Cover the pan with foil and bake for 40 minutes. Remove foil and cook 20 minutes longer.

Serves 4.

2 whole boned chicken breasts
2 cups orange juice
2 cups lightly poached salmon, flaked
⅛ cup lemon juice
½ teaspoon white pepper
¼ teaspoon chopped dill
2 cups crushed cheddar cheese crackers
¼ cup chopped green onion
1 cup melted butter

Jon's Salmon Florentine

Add oregano, red wine vinegar and Tabasco to salsa. Combine salsa mixture with chopped onion, green pepper and tomato.

Rub the fillets with butter. Lightly salt and pepper and brush with olive oil.

Place 1 fillet skin side down on aluminum foil in a large baking pan. Spread with salsa mixture. Cover with small spinach leaves and sliced vegetables. Place second fillet on top of first, skin side up. Cover with large spinach leaves.

Cover with foil and bake in a 350° oven for 50 minutes or until salmon flakes easily when tested with a fork.

Serves 10 to 12.

1 teaspoon oregano
1/4 cup red wine vinegar
1/2 teaspoon Tabasco
1 12-ounce jar salsa, medium hot
1 large red onion, thinly cut 8 slices and coarsely chop the remaining onion
1 green pepper, thinly cut 6 slices and coarsely chop the remaining pepper
1 large tomato, thinly cut 6 slices and coarsely chop the remaining tomato
2 salmon fillets, 4-5 pounds each
4 tablespoons butter
salt and pepper
olive oil
2 bunches of fresh spinach

Microwave Salmon à la Frances

Generously salt the cavity of the salmon.
Place butter slices inside salmon.
Sprinkle with juice of lemon. Add lemon
pepper, lemon peel, onion flakes, dill and
curry.

Place salmon in glass baking dish.
Cover with wine and then plastic wrap.
Puncture plastic wrap with sharp knife
in 2 or 3 places.

Place in microwave on high for 7 to 8
minutes. Remove and turn baking dish
around. Return to microwave and cook
7 to 8 minutes longer or until fish flakes
easily.

Serves 6.

1	5-pound salmon
	salt
4	tablespoons butter, sliced
1/2	lemon
1	tablespoon lemon pepper
1	tablespoon lemon peel
2	tablespoons dried onion flakes
1	tablespoon fresh dill
1/2	teaspoon curry
1	cup white wine

Seeber-Watanabe Salmon

Combine ½ of the peanut oil and the remaining ingredients. Marinate the salmon 30 minutes.

Place the fillet in a steamer and steam 20 to 30 minutes or until done. (If desired, place the fillet on a piece of cheese cloth to make removal from the steamer easier).

When fish is almost ready, heat remaining peanut oil until almost smoking.

Remove salmon from steamer and place on a serving dish. Drizzle the hot peanut oil over the fillet.

Serves 6 to 8.

4 ounces peanut oil
2 ounces hoisin sauce
2 ounces soy sauce
3 ounces ginger, crushed
¼ cup chopped scallions
¼ cup gin
1 teaspoon rice wine vinegar
1 salmon fillet

Fourth of July Salmon Barbecue

Lightly salt cavity of salmon and set aside.

Mix together rice, dried leek, bacon, tarragon, sage and ¼ cup butter. Combine with chicken broth until well blended.

Fill cavity of salmon with stuffing. Secure with skewers. (Thread skewers lengthwise to close fish and prevent piercing of foil.) Set fish on foil. Baste with melted butter and wrap securely.

Place on barbecue and cook 20 to 30 minutes on each side. Fish is done when it flakes easily when tested with a fork.

Serves 4.

1 4-5 pound whole salmon, cleaned
    salt
2 cups cooked wild rice
2 tablespoons dried leek flakes
3 slices cooked bacon, crumbled
½ teaspoon tarragon
¼ teaspoon sage
1¼ cups melted butter
1 cup chicken broth
    bamboo skewers
    foil

Dawn's Favorite Teriyaki Salmon

8 to 12 salmon steaks

Teriyaki Sauce

Combine all ingredients except salmon in a saucepan and simmer for 45 minutes. Do not boil. Make sure sugar dissolves completely. Cool.

Marinate steaks 4 hours in sauce. Barbecue steaks over hot coals until fish flakes easily when tested with a fork. Reheat Teriyaki Sauce and pour into individual ramekins to serve with salmon steaks.

Serves 8 to 12.

2	cups soy sauce
1½	cups cooking sherry
½	teaspoon garlic powder
½	teaspoon onion powder
2	teaspoons ginger
1	cup brown sugar
1¼	cups sugar

Oriental Salmon

Combine ingredients except salmon and heat stirring constantly until thickened.

Add salmon to sauce and simmer 3 to 5 minutes longer until salmon is done.

Serve immediately over white rice.

Serves 4.

2 cups cold water
2 tablespoons ketchup
2 tablespoons rice vinegar
4 tablespoons sugar
3 tablespoons plum sauce
2 carrots, cut finely into matchstick pieces
1 cucumber, cut finely into matchstick pieces
1 onion, thinly sliced
1 small salmon fillet, skinned and cut into 1-inch pieces

Columbia River Croquettes

Mix all ingredients thoroughly, except 1 cup crumbs. Shape into balls using approximately ½ cup mixture. Roll in remaining bread or cracker crumbs. Allow to stand for 10 minutes.

Brown in hot oil. Drain. Place on baking sheet and bake at 350° for approximately 30 minutes.

Serves 4 to 6.

1½ cups fine dry bread or cracker crumbs
2½ cups cooked flaked salmon
⅓ cup chopped green onion
½ cup finely chopped celery
juice of ½ lemon
1 teaspoon salt
½ teaspoon pepper
1 large egg or 2 medium eggs
½ cup mayonnaise

Polynesian Sweet-and-Sour Salmon

Sauté onion, green pepper and mushrooms in butter until tender. Drain pineapple; reserve syrup. Combine sugar, cornstarch, mustard and salt. Stir in pineapple syrup, vinegar and soy sauce. Add to onion mixture. Cook stirring constantly, until thick and clear. If needed, may be thinned with water. Add tomatoes and desired amount of pineapple chunks. Heat.

Prepare salmon according to directions for Salmon and Chips on page 142. Add to sauce. Serve immediately over rice.

For variety, add ½ package frozen cooked peas and carrots to sauce.

1 salmon fillet
1 onion, sliced
1 green pepper, cut in 1-inch squares
½ pound mushrooms, sliced
¼ cup butter
1 20-ounce can pineapple chunks
½ cup sugar
2 tablespoons corn starch
½ teaspoon dry mustard
¼ teaspoon salt
½ cup white vinegar
1 tablespoon soy sauce
2 tomatoes, cut into wedges

Salmon Stuffed Pork Chops

Cut a pocket in each chop on the side opposite the bone.

Marinate pork chops in orange juice for 3 hours.

Meanwhile, sauté green onion in 1 tablespoon butter. Combine salmon, sausage, green onion, 2 tablespoons butter, bread crumbs, lime juice, vermouth, salt and pepper. Let stand for at least 1 hour.

Remove pork chops from marinade, reserve orange juice.

Stuff each pork chop with the salmon mixture. Stand the chops in a baking dish bone side down.

Pour 2 cups of orange juice over the pork chops. Cover with aluminum foil avoiding contact with the chops. Bake in a 375° oven for 1 hour.

Meanwhile, prepare glaze mixture by combining 1/2 cup orange juice and orange marmalade. Stir over low heat until blended.

Remove foil after 1 hour of baking and baste chops with the pan juice. Bake uncovered another 20 minutes basting frequently.

After 20 minutes coat the chops with glaze mixture and place under broiler to set glaze and brown chops.

Serves 4.

4 pork chops, cut 1 1/2 inches thick with a pocket for stuffing
1 quart orange juice
3 whole green onions, thinly sliced
3 tablespoons butter, softened
2 cups cooked salmon, flaked
1/2 pound cooked pork sausage, crumbled
1 cup bread crumbs
juice of 1/2 lime
1/4 cup dry vermouth
salt
1/2 teaspoon white pepper
1 10-ounce jar orange marmalade

Peninsula Steaks

Place salmon on greased broiler rack; baste with melted butter. Salt and pepper salmon, and sprinkle lightly with lemon juice. Place broiler pan 5 inches from heat.

Broil 10 to 15 minutes or until fish flakes easily with a fork.

Serve with Lemon or Parsley Butter.

4-6 salmon steaks
butter, melted
salt
pepper
lemon juice

Lemon Butter

Add 2 to 3 tablespoons of lemon to ½ cup melted butter.

Parsley Butter

Add 2 to 3 tablespoons minced parsley to ½ cup melted butter.

Olympic Salmon Steak

*Arrange fish in a shallow baking dish.
Combine the remaining ingredients and
mix thoroughly. Pour over fish and
marinate 30 minutes.*

*Remove fish and place on a greased
broiler rack. Brush with sauce.*

*Broil 5 inches from heat about 10
minutes or until fish flakes when tested
with a fork.*

Serves 4 to 6.

4-6 salmon steaks
1 tablespoon liquid smoke
1 teaspoon salt
   dash of pepper
1 clove garlic, crushed
2 tablespoons vinegar
1/2 teaspoon paprika
1/2 teaspoon powdered mustard
3 tablespoons lemon juice
3 drops Tabasco sauce
1 teaspoon Worcestershire sauce
1/4 cup ketchup
1/4 cup butter, melted

Jackie's Salmon à la Dill

Remove head from salmon. Rinse cavity well. Sprinkle cavity with salt, then sprinkle generously with dill weed. Arrange slices of butter and onion in cavity, and cover salmon loosely with heavy-duty foil.

Barbecue fish until it is flaky and separates easily with a fork.

Serves 4 to 6.

1 whole salmon (best with 3-4 pound Coho)
8 tablespoons butter
   dill weed
   salt
1 onion, sliced

Salmon, Zucchini and Mushrooms

Sauté mushrooms in 2 tablespoons butter until tender. Remove from pan and sauté zucchini in remaining butter until tender.

In a bowl, blend sour cream, sherry, dill, salt and pepper.

Place salmon steaks in a large baking pan, cover with vegetables, and pour sauce over top. Bake at 400° for 20 minutes.

Serves 6.

6 salmon steaks
1 pound mushrooms, sliced
4 tablespoons butter
3 zucchini, thinly sliced
2 cups sour cream
3/4 cup dry sherry
1/2 teaspoon dried dill weed
1/2 teaspoon salt
1/2 teaspoon pepper

Salmon Stir Fry

In a bowl combine cornstarch and soy sauce and marinate salmon chunks for 1 hour. Heat oil in wok over high heat. Add salmon. Cook and stir until salmon is tender, about 4 minutes. Remove from oil.

Add green pepper, turnips, bok choy, mushrooms and pea pods to oil in the wok. Cook and stir for 3 minutes. Add sherry, bean sprouts and 4 teaspoons soy sauce. Return salmon to mixture with a dash of garlic powder. Cook and stir for approximately 4 minutes longer.

If desired, thicken with a little cornstarch and soy marinade.

Serve with rice.

Serves 6.

2 cups skinned uncooked salmon cut into strips 1 inch long and ½ inch wide

2 tablespoons cornstarch

2 tablespoons soy sauce for marinade

2 tablespoons peanut oil

1 green pepper, thinly sliced

2 medium sized turnips, thinly sliced

8-10 stalks bok choy, sliced

½ pound mushrooms, sliced

1 6-ounce package frozen or fresh pea pods

2 tablespoons sherry

2 cups bean sprouts

4 tablespoons soy sauce for stir fry
dash of garlic powder

Salmon à la King

Melt butter in pan. Add flour. Stirring constantly, slowly add cream and cook over medium heat until thick and bubbly. Add remaining ingredients.

Serve in patty shells, over cooked rice or toast points.

Serves 4.

2 cups cooked salmon, in chunks
3 tablespoons butter
3 tablespoons flour
1½ cups cream
¼ cup chopped pimiento
1 4-ounce can mushrooms, stems and pieces
1 cup cooked green peas salt and pepper to taste

Broccoli Salmon Casserole

In a large saucepan sauté onion in butter until tender. Add soup and heat.

Add mushrooms, cheese, dill weed, salt, pepper and lemon juice stirring until mixed well. Toss in broccoli and salmon. Pour into shallow buttered baking dish. Bake at 350° for 20 minutes.

Serves 4.

3/4 cup cooked salmon, flaked

10 ounces frozen broccoli spears (cooked)

1/2 cup chopped onion

1 tablespoon butter

1 can cream of celery soup

1 4-ounce can mushrooms, drained

3/4 cup grated parmesan cheese

1/2 teaspoon dried dill weed

1/2 teaspoon salt

1/4 teaspoon pepper

2 tablespoons lemon juice

Salmon Quiche

Crust

Sift flour, add salt, and sugar. Cut butter into flour mixture and mold into ball. Roll out and lay in quiche dish. Puncture with fork. Bake in a preheated 400° oven for 10 minutes. Remove and turn oven to 350°.

1 cup flour
6 tablespoons butter
3 tablespoons cold water
1/4 teaspoon salt
1 tablespoon sugar

Filling

Place salmon in bottom of quiche crust. Combine milk, half-and-half, and eggs.

In a separate bowl mix together remaining ingredients and place mixture on top of smoked salmon. Pour egg mixture on top. Bake approximately 45 minutes.

Let stand 15 minutes before serving.

Serves 6.

1 cup finely flaked smoked salmon
1/2 cup milk
1/2 cup half-and-half
4 eggs, beaten
1 package frozen chopped spinach, cooked
1 3-ounce package cream cheese
2 cups of shredded monterey jack cheese
1/4 teaspoon beau monde
2 tablespoons chopped onion
1/2 teaspoon salt
1/2 teaspoon thyme

Puget Sound Salmon

Season fillet with salt and pepper. Combine lime juice, garlic powder, and melted butter.

Place fillet on broiling pan skin side down. Baste with melted butter.

Broil 8 to 10 minutes or until salmon easily flakes with a fork.

Serves 4.

1 salmon fillet (from an approximately 5-pound fish)
salt
white pepper
juice of two limes
1/2 teaspoon garlic powder
1/4 cup melted butter

Broiled Salmon Italiano

Fillet salmon. Rinse.

Melt butter and add remaining ingredients. Generously baste salmon fillets.

Broil salmon 5 inches from heat for 5 minutes. Baste with remaining melted butter. Continue to broil approximately 5 more minutes or until fish flakes when tested with a fork.

Serves 6.

1 salmon, 4-6 pounds
1/4 pound butter
1/2 teaspoon garlic powder
1/2 teaspoon oregano
1/2 teaspoon rosemary
1/2 teaspoon basil

Mike's Salmon Bouillabaisse

Sauté onions and garlic in olive oil in large pot. Add all ingredients except 1 cup white wine, pepper and seafood. Cook until carrots are tender (approximately 1 hour).

Add seafood except prawns and simmer 15 minutes.

Add prawns and final cup of wine. Stir, bring to a boil, cover and cook for about 1 minute. Sprinkle with pepper.

Serves 4 to 6.

½ cup olive oil
3 cloves garlic, chopped
5 green onions, chopped
1 28-ounce can stewed tomatoes
1 soup can of clam chowder (New England style)
1½ cups water
1 cup chopped carrots
3 cups white wine
½ cup black olives, sliced
2 tablespoons dry sherry
1 teaspoon oregano
1½ teaspoons salt
½ teaspoon pepper
2 bay leaves
1 cup minced clams
2 pounds butter clams in shell
1 cup shelled crab
2 cups prawns, shelled and deveined
1 pound red snapper, skinned and cut into 1-inch pieces
1 pound halibut, skinned and cut into 1-inch pieces
1 pound salmon, skinned and cut into 1-inch pieces
1 8-ounce can tomato sauce

Salmon Paella

In a large pot sauté onion and garlic in olive oil. Add oregano, paprika, pepper, salt, saffron and pimientos. Simmer on low heat for 5 minutes to blend flavors.

Add chicken stock and base; bring to a boil. Stir in rice. Simmer about 15 minutes.

Add clams, chorizo, chicken and shrimp, continuing to simmer about 10 minutes longer until rice is tender.

Gently stir in salmon and peas; allow to heat through. Add tomatoes the last 2 minutes. Serve directly from pan with lots of green salad.

Serves 8.

- 1 medium onion, chopped
- 2 cloves garlic, minced
- 1/4 cup olive oil
- 1/2 teaspoon oregano
- 1 teaspoon paprika
- 1/2 teaspoon white pepper
- 2 teaspoons salt
  pinch of crushed saffron
- 2 tablespoons pimientos
- 4 cups of chicken stock
- 1 teaspoon chicken stock base
- 2 cups rice, uncooked
- 1 10-ounce can whole baby clams
- 1/2 pound chorizo, casing removed, sliced and cooked
- 2 cups chicken, cooked and cut into 2-inch pieces
- 1 1/2 pounds medium size raw shrimp, shelled and deveined
- 2 cups cooked salmon, broken into 1 1/2-inch chunks
- 1 cup frozen peas
- 1 tomato, cut into 1-inch pieces

Woodmere Salmon

Place salmon fillet on a cookie sheet covered with aluminum foil. Salt and pepper fillet. Liberally cover meat side of fillet with mayonnaise (it should be approximately ⅛ inch thick). Arrange butter slices and sliced olives on top of mayonnaise. Sprinkle with parsley. Squeeze lime over fillet.

Preheat oven to 500°, then turn oven off. Place salmon in oven for 30 minutes. Do not open oven door during this time.

Serves 6.

1 salmon fillet, 2-3 pounds
  mayonnaise
4 tablespoons butter, sliced
1 cup stuffed green olives, sliced
1 tablespoon parsley, minced
1 lime
  salt and pepper

Salmon Croquettes for Rosemary

Combine salmon, lemon juice, paprika, onion salt, wheat germ, bulgur, celery, green pepper, milk and 2 beaten eggs. Shape into 2-inch diameter balls.

Dip in egg mixture. Roll in bread crumbs. Let stand about 5 minutes.

Brown in hot oil. Drain. Place on baking sheet and bake at 350° for approximately 30 minutes.

Serves 4.

1½ cups cooked flaked salmon
    juice of ½ lemon
⅛ teaspoon paprika
¼ teaspoon onion salt
½ cup wheat germ
½ cup cracked wheat bulgur
½ cup chopped celery
¼ cup minced green pepper
1 cup milk
2 eggs, beaten
1 egg, slightly beaten with 1 tablespoon water
1 cup fine bread crumbs or cracker crumbs

Salmon Cecily

Crab Meat Stuffing

Melt butter in a skillet and sauté celery, onion and green pepper until tender. Add crab meat and lemon juice. Remove from stove, add bread crumbs and eggs. Stir in remaining ingredients. Let cool slightly before stuffing fish.

Coat a baking dish with oil. Lay fillets out flat, place ½ of stuffing in the middle of each fillet and roll to make it secure and neat in appearance. Place in baking dish and bake at 350° for approximately 1 hour and 20 minutes. Remove from oven. Cover with Hollandaise Sauce and serve.

Serves 8 to 10.

- 2 salmon fillets, deboned and skinned
- 4 tablespoons butter
- ½ cup minced celery
- ½ cup minced onion
- ¼ cup minced green pepper
- ½ cup fresh crab meat
- 1 tablespoon lemon juice
- 1 cup fresh bread crumbs
- 2 eggs, lightly beaten
- 1 tablespoon fresh parsley, minced
- ¼ teaspoon black pepper
- ½ teaspoon paprika
- 1 teaspoon dry mustard

Hollandaise Sauce

In top of double boiler, over 2 inches of hot but not boiling water, beat egg yolks and water together with a wire whisk until slightly thickened. Add butter, piece by piece, beating constantly after each addition, until smooth and thickened. Add cayenne pepper and lemon juice.

Makes 1 cup.

- 3 egg yolks
- 2 teaspoons water
- ¼ pound butter, cut into 4 pieces
- ⅛ teaspoon cayenne pepper
- 2 tablespoons lemon juice

Phoenecia's Salmon With Brown Rice

Melt butter in skillet. Sprinkle each steak with ¼ teaspoon salt. Lightly brown steaks on both sides. Remove from skillet and place in baking dish.

Slowly add flour to skillet and blend well. Add chicken broth and white wine slowly and stir constantly until thick and smooth.

Pour sauce over steaks. Bake in a 350° oven 30 to 40 minutes or until fish flakes when tested with a fork.

Serve with brown rice.

Serves 6.

4	tablespoons butter
6	salmon steaks
1½	teaspoons salt
4	tablespoons flour
2	cups chicken broth
1	cup white wine

Salmon Ricardo

Fillet salmon. Rinse well. Place salmon fillets skin side down in a baking dish side by side. Sprinkle fillets lightly with oregano, thyme and basil. Place 4 pieces of butter on each fillet. Squeeze ½ lemon over each piece of salmon. Place 8 pieces of bacon on each fillet and drizzle with reserved bacon fat. Spread mushrooms, onions and olives over the fish.

Combine mayonnaise and sour cream. Spread over salmon. Seal pan with foil and bake in a 350° oven for 30 minutes. Remove foil and continue baking approximately 10 minutes or until fish flakes easily when tested with a fork.

Serves 8.

1 salmon, 5-7 pounds
  oregano
  thyme
  basil
4 tablespoons butter cut into 8 pieces
1 lemon, cut in half
8 bacon strips, cut in half and cooked
2 tablespoons reserved bacon fat
½ pound mushrooms, sliced
1 cup coarsely chopped onion
1 cup coarsely chopped black olives
1½ cups mayonnaise
1½ cups sour cream

Grandma's Salmon Biscuit Bake

Sauté onion and celery in butter until tender. Stir in flour. Add milk gradually and cook until sauce is thick, stirring constantly. Stir in cream and remaining ingredients. Pour into 1 1/2 quart buttered casserole. Top with buttermilk biscuits and bake at 400° until biscuits are well done.

Serves 4.

- 2 tablespoons chopped onion
- 1/2 cup chopped celery
- 4 tablespoons butter
- 1/4 cup flour
- 1 1/4 cups milk
- 1/2 cup cream
- 1 cup flaked cooked salmon
- 2 tablespoons chopped parsley
- 1/2 teaspoon salt
- 1/8 teaspoon cayenne
- 1/4 teaspoon thyme
- 1 4-ounce can mushroom stems and pieces, drained
- 1 8-ounce can green peas, drained
- 1 package buttermilk biscuits

Cream Smoked Salmon on Toast Points

Prepare Basic White Sauce (page 156).

Add salmon and olives to white sauce. Trim crusts from bread, toast lightly and cut into triangles.

Serve salmon mixture over toast.

Serves 4.

2 cups Basic White Sauce
1½ cups smoked flaked salmon
¼ cup sliced black olives

Salmon Green Chili Croustade

Combine cream cheese, jack cheese, green chilies, green onion, cumin, garlic powder and salmon. Mix well.

Brush 1 sheet of phyllo dough at a time with butter and fold in thirds lengthwise. Place one end of folded dough in center of pizza pan extending it over the side of the pan. Butter and fold remaining dough and arrange strips in a spoke fashion evenly around pan.

Spread salmon mixture over dough. To enclose the filling, lightly twist the portion of each sheet that extends over the pan's edge. Fold the twisted sheet in half toward the center, coil the end and press into the filling. Drizzle remaining butter over the croustade.

Bake at 350° for 10 to 15 minutes or until golden brown. Serve in wedges.

Serves 6.

1 3-ounce package cream cheese, softened
1 cup monterey jack cheese, shredded
1 4-ounce can chopped green chilies
3 green onions, sliced with tops
1/2 teaspoon cumin
1/8 teaspoon garlic powder
1 cup poached, barbecued, or broiled salmon, flaked
9 sheets frozen phyllo dough, thawed
1/2 cup butter, melted

Dishwasher Salmon Steaks

Place 1 steak on each piece of foil. Season with salt, pepper, and garlic powder. Squeeze 1/2 lime over each steak. Dot with a pat of butter.

Wrap each steak envelope style with foil. Each envelope should be securely folded to prevent loss of juices while cooking.

Lay each steak side by side on top rack of empty dishwasher. Run through regular washing and drying cycle. When dishwasher shuts off, open and serve each steak immediately.

Serves 8.

8 salmon steaks, 3/4-inch thick
8 pieces heavy-duty aluminum foil
salt
pepper
garlic powder
4 small limes, cut in half
butter

Salmon Mexicana

Combine oil, vinegar, avocados, tomatoes, green pepper and onion. Add salmon and marinate in refrigerator at least 1 hour. Remove salmon.

Melt butter. Add lime juice, salt, pepper and garlic salt.

Barbecue steaks while basting with butter mixture.

Serve steaks topped with avocado mixture.

Serves 6.

1/2 cup vegetable oil
1/2 cup red wine vinegar
2 avocados, peeled and chopped
2 tomatoes, chopped
1 small green pepper, chopped finely
1 onion, chopped finely
6 salmon steaks
1 cube butter
  salt and pepper to taste
  garlic salt to taste
  juice of 2 limes

Salmon Wellington

Sprinkle fillet with lemon juice.

Combine mayonnaise, horseradish and dill. Set aside.

Roll bread dough in rectangle 1 inch larger than salmon fillet. Place fillet on dough. Spread with mayonnaise mixture and top with black olives.

Roll dough and seal each end. Place on greased baking sheet. Bake in a 350° oven for 45 minutes or until golden brown.

Slice and serve with Mustard Sauce (page 145).

Serves 8 to 10.

1 salmon fillet, boned and skinned
1 lemon
2 cups mayonnaise
2 tablespoons horseradish
1/2 teaspoon dill
1 loaf frozen bread dough, thawed
1/3 cup black olives, sliced

Cheryl's Salmon Rice Loaf

Combine all ingredients and blend thoroughly. Place in a greased loaf pan. Bake 1 hour at 350°.

Serve with Hollandaise Sauce (page 155) or Parsley Sauce (page 150).

1 cup cooked rice
1/2 cup cracker crumbs
1 cup milk
1 small onion, finely chopped
1 celery stalk, finely chopped
1 small carrot, grated
3 cups cooked salmon, flaked
2 large eggs, beaten
1/2 teaspoon salt
1/4 teaspoon white pepper

Mathilde's Salmonburgers

In a large mixing bowl combine onion, salmon, broth, bread crumbs, eggs, parsley, mustard and salt.

Shape into 6 patties. Roll in crushed cracker crumbs and fry in hot vegetable oil until golden brown.

Serves 6.

1/2	cup chopped onion
	vegetable oil
3	cups cooked salmon, flaked
1/3	cup chicken broth
1/3	cup dry bread crumbs
2	eggs, beaten
1/4	cup chopped parsley
1	teaspoon powdered mustard
1/2	teaspoon salt
	cheddar cheese crackers, crushed fine

Tofino Swell Salmon

Place salmon fillets skin side down in shallow baking dish. Sprinkle with juice of limes, coriander, and salt and pepper to taste. Cover liberally with honey. Sprinkle with brown sugar. Place slices of butter on brown sugar.

Bake in a 375° oven for approximately 20 minutes or until fish flakes easily when tested with a fork. Baste frequently during baking with pan juices.

When fish is done, place under broiler for 2 minutes. Serve with sauce from baking dish.

Serves 6 to 8.

2 salmon fillets
2 limes
1/2 teaspoon coriander
   salt and pepper to taste
2 cups honey
1 cup brown sugar
1/4 pound butter, sliced in 6-8 pieces

Salmon Marylou

Butter ring mold or bundt pan. Line with sole.

In a food processor combine the remaining ingredients. Blend until mixture is smooth and creamy. Pour into mold.

Fold sole fillets over the top, overlapping to cover the mousse mixture. Dot with butter. Place mold in baking pan and add 2 inches of water. Bake in a 375° oven for 30 minutes.

Remove mold from pan and cool for 2 to 3 minutes. Invert on serving dish. Garnish with parsley or lettuce.

Slice and serve with Mustard Sauce (page 145).

Serves 4-6.

* You will need enough sole to arrange in a ring mold or bundt pan.

1	salmon fillet, approximately 1½ pounds, skinned, boned and cut into cubes
6-8	fillets of sole*
2	eggs
½	lime
½	teaspoon white pepper
¼	teaspoon salt
½	cup green onion, minced

Salmon Oscar

Roll fillets in flour. Combine eggs and water in a bowl and dip fillets into mixture. Roll in flour again. Brown on both sides in butter over medium heat, cooking approximately 10 minutes or until salmon is done.

Meanwhile, cook the asparagus spears until just tender.

Place 1 salmon fillet on each serving plate. Top with 3 spears of asparagus and a crab leg. Pour warm Hollandaise Sauce (page 155) over salmon and serve.

Serves 6.

6 6-ounce salmon fillets, skinned
2 eggs
2 tablespoons water
flour
½ cup butter
18 asparagus spears
6 crab legs, shelled
Hollandaise Sauce

Salmon Pizza

Roll your favorite pizza dough into a circle and place on pizza pan.

Spread the tomato sauce on the dough. Layer with mozzarella cheese, then salmon, black olives, green pepper, onion and mushrooms. Season with oregano and salt and pepper to taste. Top with parmesan cheese.

Bake in a 450° oven for 15 to 20 minutes. Serve immediately.

Serves 4.

pizza dough
2 cups cooked salmon, flaked
1 small can tomato sauce
12 ounces mozzarella cheese, thinly sliced
1/2 cup black olives, thinly sliced
1/2 cup green pepper, finely chopped
1/2 cup onion, finely chopped
1 small can mushrooms, thinly sliced
1/4 teaspoon oregano
salt
pepper
1/2 cup parmesan cheese, grated

E.R. Rogers' Baked Salmon Supreme

Place salmon in a small baking dish skin side down. Cover with wine, butter and juice of the lemon. Spread mustard evenly on top of each fillet.

Cover pan with foil and bake in a pre-heated 400° oven for 8 to 10 minutes. Remove from oven. Cover salmon with cheese and sprinkle with dill. Return to oven until cheese has melted. Place 4 shrimp on each fillet and serve immediately.

Serves 2.

2 8-ounce salmon fillets
4 ounces white wine
4 ounces butter
1 lemon
4 ounces muenster cheese, grated
4 teaspoons dill
1 tablespoon Dijon mustard
8 shrimp, shelled, deveined and cooked

Croquettes Marrero

Thoroughly mix all ingredients except bread crumbs and shrimp. Shape into balls around a large shrimp or prawn with the tail extending. Roll in fine bread or cracker crumbs. Allow to sit for 10 minutes.

Brown in hot oil. Drain. Place on baking sheet and bake at 350° for approximately 30 minutes.

Serves 4 to 6.

- 1 cup fine dry bread or cracker crumbs
- 2½ cups cooked flaked salmon
- ⅓ cup chopped green onion
- ½ cup finely chopped celery
   juice of ½ lemon
- 1 teaspoon salt
- ½ teaspoon pepper
- 1 large egg or 2 medium eggs
- ½ cup mayonnaise
- 12 large shrimp or prawns, shelled and deveined

Salmon Almondine

Roll fillets in flour. Combine eggs and water in a bowl and dip fillets into mixture. Roll in flour again.

Brown on both sides in butter over medium heat, cooking approximately 10 minutes or until salmon is done.

Transfer onto a warm platter and cover with Madeira Sauce (page 152). Spoon almonds over sauce.

Serves 4.

4 individual serving-size salmon fillets, skinned
2 eggs
2 tablespoons water
  flour
1/2 cup butter
1 cup blanched almonds
  Madeira Sauce

Westport Salmon and Chips

Combine flour, beer and oil. Fold in egg whites. Coat strips of salmon in batter. Deep fry until golden brown. Serve with tartar sauce, lemon, cole slaw and your favorite french fries.

For an English flavor try malt vinegar on your salmon and chips.

Serves 4.

1 cup flour
¾ cup beer
1 tablespoon salad oil
3 egg whites, beaten stiff
salmon fillet, skinned and cut into 1-inch by 2-inch strips

SAUCES

Mustard Sauce

Prepare Basic White Sauce (page 156). Add remaining ingredients and stir over low heat until butter melts and is well blended.

Basic White Sauce
2 tablespoons prepared mustard
¼ cup butter
1 tablespoon Madeira

Cucumber Sauce

Slice cucumber lengthwise and scoop out seeds. Grate and drain. (Food processor works the best to grate.)

Combine remaining ingredients and add grated cucumber. Chill.

Serve in place of tartar sauce on your favorite salmon dish.

1 cucumber (unpeeled)
½ cup sour cream
¼ cup mayonnaise
¼ cup grated onion
2 teaspoons vinegar
2 tablespoons minced parsley
 salt and pepper to taste

Remoulade

Mix all ingredients thoroughly. Chill for at least 6 hours.

Stir and serve over chilled cooked salmon.

- 1 cup mayonnaise
- 3 hard cooked eggs, chopped
- 2 teaspoons chopped capers
- 1 teaspoon prepared mustard
- 1 tablespoon tarragon wine vinegar
- 1 teaspoon lemon juice
- 1 teaspoon garlic powder
- 1 tablespoon finely minced parsley
- 2 tablespoons finely minced green onion
- 1 teaspoon prepared horseradish
- 1/4 teaspoon savory

Big D's Awesome Sauce 'Em

Sauté chopped onion in butter until tender. Add remaining ingredients except lemon and simmer 10 to 20 minutes on low heat.

Just prior to basting the fish, add the juice and pulp of the lemons. Simmer another 5 minutes.

This is an excellent sauce for barbecued salmon fillets or steaks. Generously baste on fish or steaks while cooking on the barbecue.

1 white onion (preferably Walla Walla Sweet), chopped
1 cube butter
2 cups packed brown sugar
¼ cup molasses
¼ cup honey
1 tablespoon Worcestershire sauce
1 tablespoon mustard
salt and pepper to taste
garlic powder to taste
3 lemons

Garden Green Sauce

Wash spinach and watercress leaves.
Place the wet spinach and watercress
leaves in a small saucepan. Cover and
simmer gently 4 to 5 minutes. Add
tarragon and chervil and simmer 2
minutes longer.

Remove from heat and place in blender
or food processor. Puree until smooth.
Blend in mayonnaise to desired
consistency. Cover and chill 2 to 4 hours.

Serve this sauce in place of tartar sauce
with your favorite salmon dish.

1 bunch fresh spinach
1 bunch fresh
   watercress
   pinch of tarragon
1 teaspoon dry chervil
   mayonnaise

Teriyaki Sauce

Combine all ingredients in a saucepan and simmer for 45 minutes. Do not boil. Make sure sugar dissolves completely. Cool.

2 cups soy sauce
1½ cups cooking sherry
½ teaspoon garlic powder
½ teaspoon onion powder
2 teaspoons ginger
1 cup brown sugar
1¼ cups sugar

Catherine's Choice

Combine all ingredients in double boiler and place over simmering water. Cover and heat until butter is melted.

Serve over baked, barbecued or broiled salmon.

4 tablespoons butter
1 clove garlic, crushed
4 tablespoons soy sauce
2 tablespoons prepared mustard
½ cup ketchup
    dash of Worcestershire sauce

Parsley Sauce

Melt butter over low heat. Slowly add flour and blend well. Add cream and stir constantly until thick and smooth. Blend in parsley. Salt and pepper to taste.

This sauce is excellent served over salmon loaf.

1 tablespoon butter
1 tablespoon flour
1 cup cream
   salt and white pepper to taste
2-3 tablespoons fresh minced parsley

Salmon Bearnaise Sauce for Vegetables

Prepare Basic White Sauce as on page 156. Add remaining ingredients and heat thoroughly.

Serve over broccoli, cauliflower, asparagus, Brussels sprouts or your favorite vegetable.

1 cup Basic White Sauce
1 cup sour cream
¼ cup Madeira wine
⅛ teaspoon white pepper
1 teaspoon horseradish
½ teaspoon coriander
1 cup smoked salmon, finely flaked

Madeira Sauce

Prepare Basic White Sauce as on page 156. Add remaining ingredients and heat thoroughly.

Serves 4.

1 cup Basic White Sauce
1 cup sour cream
1/4 cup Madeira wine
1/8 teaspoon white pepper
1 teaspoon horseradish
1/2 teaspoon coriander

Raspberry Sauce

Cook raspberry wine or vinegar with green onions until reduced to 2 tablespoons.

Add cream, stir over low heat until once again reduced to 2 tablespoons.

Add butter, and continue to stir over low heat until thickened. Add jam.

Fabulous over poached, barbecued or broiled salmon.

1/2 cup raspberry wine or vinegar
1/4 cup minced green onion
4 tablespoons whipping cream
1/2 cup butter
2 tablespoons raspberry jam

Cheese-Squid Sauce

Cover squid with 2 cups of milk in a medium saucepan. Bring to a near boil. Remove from heat and strain liquid into top of double boiler. Place over simmering water. Add garlic powder, cheese, mustard and butter to milk.

Dissolve flour in 1/3 cup milk. Add slowly to cheese sauce, stirring constantly until thickened. Add salt and pepper to taste.

This sauce is great with your favorite salmon loaf.

Note: Use squid in the preparation of other dishes or as an appetizer.

1 pound squid, cleaned and skinned
2 1/3 cups milk
1/8 teaspoon garlic powder
4 slices American cheese, diced
1/2 teaspoon prepared mustard
3 tablespoons flour
1/4 cup butter
salt
pepper

Dill Sauce

Combine mayonnaise, sour cream, dill weed and garlic powder. Let chill several hours.

This sauce is delicious with chilled leftover salmon.

½ cup mayonnaise
½ cup sour cream
1 heaping tablespoon dill weed
   dash of garlic powder

Tarragon Sauce

Blend ingredients in a small bowl. Cover and chill 2 to 4 hours.

This sauce is particularly good over poached salmon.

½ cup mayonnaise
2 teaspoons lemon juice
½ teaspoon crushed fresh tarragon
   pinch of grated lemon rind

Hollandaise Sauce

In top of double boiler, over 2 inches of hot but not boiling water, beat egg yolks and water together with a wire whisk, until slightly thickened.

Add butter, piece by piece, beating constantly after each addition, until smooth and thickened. Add cayenne pepper and lemon juice.

Makes 1 cup.

3 egg yolks
2 teaspoons water
1/4 pound butter, cut into 4 pieces
1/8 teaspoon cayenne pepper
2 tablespoons lemon juice

Basic White Sauce

Melt butter over low heat. Slowly add
flour and blend well. Add milk slowly
and stir constantly until thick and
smooth. Salt and pepper to taste.

2 tablespoons butter
2 tablespoons flour
1 cup milk
  salt to taste
  white pepper to taste

SMOKED
SALMON

Gracious Smoked Salmon

Fillet salmon. Cut fillets into strips approximately 3 inches by 5 inches.

Place fish skin side down in a large shallow pan. Sprinkle liberally with salt. Let stand 8 to 12 hours or overnight.

Rinse each piece of fish, pat dry with a paper towel and allow to air dry skin side up on a rack for 1 hour. While fish is air drying, cut brown paper the size of the fish pieces.

Place fish skin side down on paper. Liberally baste each piece with maple syrup. Place in smoker.

Baste with syrup 3 or 4 times during first 4 hours of smoking. Continue to smoke 4 to 8 hours or until done. Use 2 to 3 pans of alder or fruitwood chips during smoking process.

Remove from smoker. Cool and peel off paper. This will also remove the skin. The fish will be ready to serve or refrigerate until ready to use. Refrigerates well for 2 to 3 weeks.

salmon
non-iodized rock salt or kosher salt
pure maple syrup
brown wrapping paper
alder or fruitwood chips

Apricot Smoked Salmon

Fillet salmon. Cut fillets into strips approximately 3 inches by 5 inches.

Place fish skin side down in a large shallow pan. Sprinkle liberally with salt. Let stand 8 to 12 hours or overnight.

Rinse each piece of fish, pat dry with a paper towel and allow to air dry skin side up on a rack for 1 hour. While fish is air drying, cut brown paper the size of the fish pieces.

Place fish skin side down on paper. Liberally baste each piece with apricot syrup. Place in smoker.

Baste with syrup 3 or 4 times during first 4 hours of smoking. Continue to smoke 4 to 8 hours or until done. Use 2 to 3 pans of alder or fruitwood chips during smoking process.

Remove from smoker. Cool and peel off paper. This will also remove the skin. The fish will be ready to serve or refrigerate until ready to use. Refrigerates well for 2 to 3 weeks.

salmon
non-iodized rock salt
or kosher salt
apricot syrup
brown wrapping
paper
alder or fruitwood
chips

Traditional Smoked Salmon

Fillet salmon. Cut fillets into strips approximately 3 inches by 5 inches.

Fill a dishpan 1/3 full of cold water. Add salt, brown sugar and a generous amount of garlic salt. Brine salmon 6 to 10 hours depending on thickness. Remove fish from brine and allow to air dry skin-side up on a rack for 1 hour.

Place in smoker skin-side down. Smoke 10 to 12 hours or until done. Use 2 to 3 pans of hickory or alder chips during the smoking process.

Remove from smoker. The fish will be ready to serve or refrigerate until ready to use. Refrigerates well for 2 to 3 weeks.

salmon
1 cup salt
1 cup brown sugar
garlic salt
hickory or alder chips

Sweet Smoked Salmon

For a sweeter taste to your smoked salmon, follow directions for traditional smoked salmon above. While the salmon is air drying, rub brown sugar into each piece.

INDEX